PRAISE FOR

The Art & Science
of Facilitation

"Marsha Acker is the finest facilitator I know. In this eye-opening book, she activates the "how-to-be" of becoming an accomplished facilitator. Getting right to the heart of it, she reveals the cornerstones that both support and challenge you to step into the mindset of a facilitator, and she matches that challenge with down-to-earth practices you can start using now. If you have been wondering why the latest facilitation tool hasn't quite "done it" or you feel disheartened by the lack of real conversation, this book is for you."

— Lyssa Adkins, Agile & Leadership Coach and
author of *Coaching Agile Teams*

"Drawing on her years as a facilitation and leadership trainer, Marsha Acker has written a guide to agile facilitation that is clear, engaging, and smart. Acker teaches us the mechanics and mindsets we need, and just as importantly, why these skills matter so much. Every voice in an organization matters, and Acker shows us how to hear each one."

—Douglas Stone and Sheila Heen,
co-authors of the best-sellers,
Difficult Conversations and *Thanks for the Feedback.*

"For facilitators wanting powerful results, this book reveals the crucial lessons behind truly engaging all voices."
— Tricia Broderick, Founder, Ignite Insight + Innovation

"Great facilitation doesn't just happen, or come from knowledge alone. In this book, Marsha brilliantly shares how facilitation is an inside-out practice, starting with the facilitator's own belief system, awareness and development. If you are an Agile Coach and want to develop your competency to work more deeply with systemic challenges and stuck patterns in your organizations – this book is meant for you! "
— Michele Madore, Principal, Trans4mation and co-author of *Agile Transformation: Using the Integral Agile Transformation Framework to Think and Lead Differently.*

"Great facilitation is usually the missing ingredient to productive collaboration and inclusive leadership. I've been very fortunate to have experienced firsthand how Marsha's approach to facilitation can transform individuals and teams and build a culture of collaboration and dialogue. This book beautifully reflects Marsha's expertise and experience and is a must-read for both new and experienced coaches and leaders who want to grow their leadership range and stand against dysfunctional communication patterns. You'll walk away from this book with practical tips you can implement immediately and a deeper awareness of how you can successfully "stand in the storm."
—Ahmed Sidky, Ph.D., Head of Business Agility, Riot Games

"A great book for new facilitators starting out. Marsha not only offers fantastic practical guidance for skill-building but also takes you into the hidden aesthetics of facilitation. She offers her model for how to navigate this territory, with all the potential that exists to transform what is otherwise so often illusory and difficult to grasp. A wonderful resource!"

— Dr. Sarah Hill,
Co-owner of Dialogix Ltd and author of *Where Did You Learn To Behave Like That* and *The Tao of Dialogue*

"Facilitation is perhaps the key skill for anyone who cares about organizational effectiveness. And yet it calls upon leaders to reach deeply into themselves if they are to bring any degree of mastery to the craft of facilitation—which is not so easy. *The Art and Science of Facilitation* provides a powerful roadmap that integrates *practice* with *being*, *science* with *art* in a way that is at once accessible and profound. With every sentence I read in this book, I can sense both the deep wisdom of a sage and the down-in-the-trenches experience of a highly seasoned practitioner. Skipping the "filler" and bypassing niceties, the book pulls no punches. Masterful facilitation may not be easy, but with Marsha's kind and assured guidance, it becomes totally doable."

—Michael Hamman, author of *Evolvagility: Growing an Agile Leadership Culture from the Inside Out*

"I know from first-hand experience that Marsha is a master facilitator—fortunately for the reader, in this book she has distilled this mastery into a highly actionable set of perspectives and practices for facilitating groups. Having taught many hundreds of agile facilitators in my career, I would love to have had this book to offer them after class. You'd do well to invest your time here."

— Michael Spayd, The Collective Edge,
co-author of *Agile Transformation: Using the Integral Agile Transformation Framework to Think and Lead Differently*

"The Art and Science of Facilitation is the definitive book for anyone holding a facilitation role - whether that is your career or a role you sometimes play. Through personal stories, practical lessons, and informative scenarios, Marsha gives you the tools you need to "manage yourself" and create a valuable and effective collaboration experience for everyone. This book has personally helped me identify areas of improvement in my own facilitation and I look forward to applying some of the tools to do so. I hope you find the same when you read it."

— Evan Leybourn,
CEO & Cofounder, Business Agility Institute

"There are plenty of books out there on coaching and facilitation practices but this book really captures the essence of what it means to be in the facilitation stance. It is a must read for anybody coaching or leading an Agile team regardless of whether they are new to the role or a seasoned professional. I have been lucky enough to learn from Marsha directly as well as work alongside her in providing feedback and assessment to Agile coaches. This book has bottled the expert knowledge she has in this field and has made it available for all to learn and grow from."

— Craig Smith, Global Agility Lead, SoftEd

"When people ask for me for references on facilitation, I give them a list, with the caveat that when Marsha Acker writes her book, it will replace all these references. I can stop saying that now! The Art and Science of Facilitation is an indispensable guide that beautifully reveals the real soul of facilitation; the things no one teaches, but you know it when you feel it. Marsha breaks facilitation down into tangible practices you can start using today, and continue to use to deepen your level of mastery. Keep this book with you at all times."

— Jardena London,
founder of Rosetta Agile and Souls@Work,
author of *Transformational Leadership:
Connecting the Spiritual and Practical*

"Marsha has created the pathway that can help facilitators take agile teams deeper into their intrinsic wisdom for better outcomes. Approaching facilitation as both an art and a science, she lays out an approach that is the 'doorway to collective intelligence, better decisions, alignment, shared understanding, and commitment.' This is a must-read for collaborative leaders who enjoy the complex dance of facilitation polarities, who want to honor the wisdom of their teams; and who want to enable individuals to be part of something greater than themselves."

—Sanjiv Augustine,
Founder and CEO, LitheSpeed LLC

THE ART & SCIENCE OF FACILITATION

*How to Lead Effective
Collaboration with Agile Teams*

MARSHA ACKER

TeamCatapult Publishing

Cover Design: Alex Thomas with Monica Haynes
Illustrations/Interior design: Colleen Sheehan/Alchemy Book Design

Printed in the United States of America

For Don and Lauren,
you bring laughter, love,
and joy to my life.

TABLE OF CONTENTS

INTRODUCTION

Have we forgotten how to communicate and collaborate with others, or did we just never learn?

The pace and sheer quantity of complex decisions we're trying to make each day—our need to constantly innovate amid continuous change—create conditions that make workplace collaboration necessary. Unfortunately, they also create the conditions that make collaboration challenging.

It's a fool's errand. The very thing that we need more of—a collaborative work environment—is the very thing we feel like we don't have time to cultivate.

More often than not, what we do instead is what my colleague Ben Tinker calls "collaboration theater." We create artificial space where we go through the motions of something *resembling* collaboration, but we do it in a quick, cursory manner. We don't feel like we have any more time to give the process. Besides, when we don't actually reach a decision by consensus, we know that the leader will just step in and make the decision for us anyway.

True collaboration is when new ideas are generated from conversation. We do a whole lot of things when we come together, but very seldom do we truly carve out space to be creative, to tap into the collective intelligence, and to think together. Yet it is within truly collaborative spaces that teams discover solutions to their most complex problems.

This book is about using facilitation to foster collaborative, generative conversations in team settings.

Facilitation is about taking a stand. It's about creating the space for what's needed to help people show up as their most naturally creative selves, voice their point of view authentically, hear different perspectives, develop a shared vision for the future, and decide on a direction forward. Facilitation does not fall for impossible outcomes in unrealistic time frames. It does not stand for unequal participation. It is for creating engaging and connected spaces where all voices are heard.

Once a team has experienced facilitation done well, they will not want to live without it.

> "Facilitation is the art of leading people through processes of agreed-upon outcomes in a manner that encourages participation, ownership, and creativity from all involved."
> ~The Grove Consultants International

AGILE FACILITATION

While speaking to the craft of facilitation broadly, this book is anchored in the world of agility.

The concept of agile facilitation originated when the needs of complex work environments were no longer being met by the way we'd been working. Responding to the changing needs of the software development industry in particular, a group of thought leaders gathered to have a different kind of conversation. They asked, "What would make this better?" Their answer was the Agile Manifesto. In 2010, Lyssa Adkins helped define facilitation and coaching even further by publishing the groundbreaking book, *Coaching Agile Teams*. Since then, the discipline of agile facilitation has continued to evolve.

Agility creates a tension in our organizations that forces us to look at how we lead and work together. It is the basis for a concept of teamwork that values individuals and interactions over processes and tools. Coaching agility in teams draws on the disciplines of professional facilitation, professional coaching, teaching, and team development to help teams adapt to change at the individual and team levels. It is an emerging discipline that requires a certain level of competency and expertise in each of the disciplines it draws from.

For those in the agile world, welcome! You may find that you play a unique role in your team as you attempt to straddle the concept of remaining neutral while also being a member of the team in some capacity. This dual role creates a natural tension unique to agile coaching—a tension between content and process. This book provides a clear path forward in your own practice.

For those who are new to agile or have never heard of it before, the facilitation concepts covered in this book are still for you. The success of any facilitation is more about who you are and how you are being in the room than it is about what tool or technique you use. The chapters to come will help you develop your self-awareness in facilitation so that you can understand and feel in control of how you show up.

This book is not an introduction to agility. It is an introduction to using facilitation to support the development of high-performing teams who are getting work done in a collaborative and adaptive manner.

FACILITATION IS BOTH AN ART AND A SCIENCE

If you find yourself responsible for leading teams—of any size—toward better outcomes, then chances are you have stepped into the role of facilitator at some point.

But what does it mean to be a facilitator? Even though the word is frequently used, its meaning varies enormously in different settings. Sometimes it's used to describe the person who booked the room, ordered the pizza, and invited everyone to the meeting. Other times, the facilitator is the person who makes the decisions and leads the meeting. However, while a facilitator might do the former, a true facilitator would not do the latter. A facilitator would not be the one making the decisions unless they also have another set of responsibilities, such as being the team leader or manager. If that is the case, the decision gets made while they are wearing their other hat.

Before we begin to talk about facilitation, let's align on what we mean when we use the word "facilitator."

> A facilitator is an individual who uses self-awareness, self-management, group awareness, and group process to enable teams to access their collective intelligence in order to achieve their desired outcomes.

In other words, facilitation is not just about what tool or technique you are applying. Just as much, if not more, it is about what you believe, who you are being in the moment, and what you see and sense in the group.

I would much rather be a participant in a group that is being led by a grounded, self- and group-aware facilitator than someone who has a toolkit packed with techniques but no idea

4

about their personal impact in the room. Why? Because the grounded, aware facilitator will be able to adapt almost any technique to fit the group, while the person armed only with the toolkit will struggle to engage the group in meaningful dialogue or decision-making—regardless of the tool they choose.

Now, you might be thinking, "I lead meetings all the time, so I don't need to learn how to facilitate. Of all the things I could spend my time learning, facilitation is low on my priority list."

But here's what you need to consider:

- Are your meetings effective?
- Do they get to the group's desired outcomes?
- Are difficult topics surfaced and talked about within the group, or do they go "offline"?
- Do decisions stick, or do you revisit the same conversation each week?

If your meetings are working, then great! If not, are you willing to look at how you, as a meeting leader, might be playing a part in the breakdown?

Facilitation matters. It is more than just sticky notes and dots for voting. It is a craft. Our reality is socially constructed, which means that how we talk to and with one another—the words we use, the way we speak, the metaphors that describe our ideas—all inform the effectiveness or ineffectiveness of our work. Teams do not typically have the ability or skill to talk with each other productively without practice. This is the promise of facilitation.

Facilitation is both an art and a science. The science comes from what we know about how people think—how groups behave and teams develop. The art is how the facilitator learns to dance in the moment—seeing what's happening in a group, hearing what's behind the way the group talks with one another, listening for what's not being said, and letting the magic of the group's collective intelligence organically emerge.

If you're ready to step up as a true facilitator—someone with range in their leadership who can take a stand against dysfunctional patterns in communication and collaboration—then this book is for you.

LETTING GO OF THE HERO

It's time to reframe the way we think about leadership. The old metaphors and visuals that have one person (the hero) charging ahead, clearing the path, and setting the direction while others passively follow along no longer fits with the current world of work.

We do still need people to point in a direction, but we also need to hear all voices. The world of work is too complex and moves too fast for any one person to keep up with everything or have all the answers. Think about your relationship to your cell phone. New versions of software are released to our phones multiple times a day, which means that we're constantly learning small new ways of accomplishing tasks that we used to perform differently. The pace of change can feel overwhelming, and that's just one device! Now, scale that rate of fast-paced change to a team or business. Teamwork and collaboration are imperative to keep up with change, innovate accordingly, and move forward.

That's why we need to tap into the collective intelligence that resides within the group.

If you have ever participated in a meeting without facilitation, you likely felt it on some level. Maybe you felt frustrated and thought it was all a waste of time. Maybe you wondered why you even had to meet. Perhaps you felt like nobody cared what you thought—or like no one was listening anyway. Meetings without facilitation often leave people feeling dismissed, stepped on or frustrated, and like the same thing is being talked about over and over again with no new progress.

By contrast, if you have ever had the opportunity to work with or be a part of a meeting led by a skilled facilitator, then you likely left that meeting feeling accomplished, clear, and focused. Whether or not you were aware that the person was facilitating or understood what they were doing, the experience might have felt a bit like magic: somehow you got where you needed to get in a manner that felt productive.

If you're lucky enough to have experienced facilitation done really well, you might have found yourself saying, "What just happened in there? That was awesome!" or, "How do we do that again?!"

But efforts to recreate that great experience can feel really frustrating. You will not find a playbook, a checklist, or a series of steps that you, too, can follow and get the same result. Why? Because the facilitation you experienced will have been both an art and a science. It will likely have included the facilitator "leading from the front" by setting a direction, "leading from behind" with questions and curiosity, and "leading together," offering ideas but not assertions and providing clarity without judgement.[1]

What you likely experienced was leadership through facilitation—a process of asking for other perspectives and being willing to inquire into others' ideas. What you did *not* experience was the traditional view of leadership in which one person set the direction and expected everyone to follow along.

---

1   For more on the idea of leading from the front, from behind, and together, see Karen and Henry Kimsey-House, *Co-Active Leadership: Five Ways to Lead* (Oakland: Berrett-Koehler Publishers, 2015).

So, why is it often so hard to cultivate and enact the kind of leadership that feels this open and generative?

I've taught hundreds of leaders the skills of facilitation and have found that one of the biggest barriers to developing this model of leadership is the fact that it challenges three fundamental beliefs:

- **"We don't have time for all this facilitation stuff. We need to get something *done!*"**
  There is strong power in the belief that organizations are about results and action. The subtext is that talking and thinking together is *not* action—that talking and listening to one another wastes time. In fact, this belief is so fundamental to many organizations that leaders are willing to risk six months of waste in order to avoid just four to six hours of "talk."

- **"I'm the one who will be held responsible and accountable, so I don't need others telling me what to do."**
  The subtext of this common belief is that the "leader" knows best and already has all the answers. Others might very well have a vision— and the leader might even like the vision!—but the assumption is that only the leader has the ability to see and catch all the complications that may arise.

- **"To ask others is to give up my power."**
  This belief is fairly straightforward. In the competitive world of business, many believe that

expressing anything other than the traditional top-down leadership model is tantamount to expressing weakness and relinquishing power.

Collaboration can be a powerful process. At its best, it's the doorway to collective intelligence, better decisions, alignment, shared understanding, and commitment. But when people convene to get work done, they often do everything *but* make progress. We have a habit of getting in our own way when it comes to what we want to accomplish.

Letting go of our beliefs about what leadership "should" look like is the first step to clearing a path forward for better facilitation and, ultimately, better results.

DON'T RUN DOWN THE ROAD—GET IN THE CAR!

I'm pretty sure that if someone took the time to run the numbers, the cost of meeting time in today's organizations would appall executive teams.

Left to their own devices, wheels just spin. They need traction, they need direction, and they need to work together. This is why a facilitator is one of the most crucial positions—and it's missing in most organizations. Facilitators play a critical role in moving groups toward productive solutions and agreed-upon outcomes.

Here are just a few examples of where skilled facilitators make all the difference:

- Leading a high-stakes meeting with multiple stakeholders to align on a plan that everyone will actively support

- Getting a team in breakdown into conversation so they can move forward in a positive direction
- Planning the work to be done for the next few weeks
- Creating a shared vision and goals for a new team
- Hosting meetings with the top team and leading them to consensus
- Sorting out a heated debate between two teams about how they will work together

But even with a facilitator in place, it takes time to shift the culture of meetings—especially in an environment where unproductive, unsatisfying meetings have long been the norm.

> A question I frequently get asked by agile facilitators and coaches is, "How do you get people to come to a meeting and participate when they don't want to?" The short answer is, you invite them and ask them what they need.

People have to know what they will get out of the meeting, why you're having it, and what you need from them. Even better, you've asked them what *they* need to get out of the meeting. And then you take the time to show that their voices, their perspectives, and their time are all being honored in the group setting.

So, yes, effective group collaboration does take time to develop. It requires a skilled facilitator and, frequently, a culture shift. But what takes *more* time is trying to figure it all out through ineffective meetings.

Once, long ago, I stopped into my boss's office while overwhelmed with the amount of work on my plate. He offered a couple of strategies to help. My response to his suggestions was to argue that none of them would work in our current level of crisis.

He said, "You're running down the road, telling me you're too busy to get in the car."

He was right.

THIS IS A BOOK ABOUT HOW TO *BE*—NOT WHAT TO DO

The role of a facilitator is to be a safari guide through the jungle of opinions, biases, interpersonal conflict, personal fears, organizational fears, and sub-surface group dynamics that are present in any group setting.

As facilitators, whenever we convene a group, we start by distinguishing two things: the "What" and the "How."

The "What" is the content—the topic of the group meeting. The "How" is the collection of structures, methods, techniques, and frameworks we'll use to help a group access its full collective intelligence. The "How" is the complex, nuanced world of structural dynamics and communication at play in the room. It is how the group members are behaving and how they are communicating with one another.

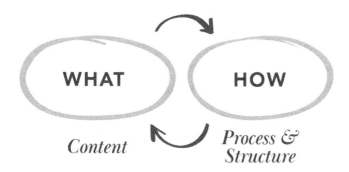

WHAT — HOW

Content — *Process & Structure*

I see new facilitators get really excited by the addition of new tools and techniques to their "Process" toolkit. I do, too. But this book is not about the "Process." While tools, templates, and exercises are all VERY helpful (I myself would sometimes be lost without them), they are not what will make you a more effective facilitator. Skilled facilitation is more nuanced than that. It starts with what you believe and how you think—because how we think is how we lead when we step in front of a group.

Effective collaboration—navigating differences of opinion, points of view, and perspectives in a way that makes space for all voices and achieves the desired outcomes—is complex. But the core of this complexity does not lie in the tools or techniques we choose to use or whether we are facilitating a small team or a five-hundred-person event. The core of the complexity is *mindset.*

What does this mean? It means that if I believe my role is all about the range of tools and techniques I have at my fingertips, I am holding a very linear and "me"-centric view of facilitation. It means that I believe a group's success will be dependent on the number of tools and techniques I can bring to the table. When I bring forward a tool to use in a meeting, therefore, I do so with a narrow focus and less intentionality. I may be able to choose a specific tool in an effort to meet a specific need, but my choice of tools is always informed by what I think the *outcome* of using it will be. It is cause-and-effect thinking.

But what we know about human systems is that they are not that simple. They are not that linear.

So, instead, if I adopt the mindset (the belief) that the group is a system and that my role as facilitator is part of, not separate from, that system, I can take a wider and deeper perspective on how my intentions and actions will impact the group's outcomes. My actions will shift from doing something "to the team" to co-creating something *with* the team. I'll be able to see the whole system (complexity thinking), the dynamics that are playing out in the room, and the dynamics and factors at play outside the room. I'll be able to see actions as non-linear. With this mindset, I know that my choice to bring a certain tool or technique forward will be informed by more perspectives than just my own. I'll be using my toolkit with more intentionality because I'll be seeing systemic patterns. And I'll be able to intervene in ways that will help the group produce better outcomes because I will recognize—and help the group recognize—that outcomes may not be linear.

In short, what makes an effective facilitator is *not* what's in their toolkit, it's the mindset that informs how they *use* their toolkit. Or, simply: **How we think is how we act.**

So, this book is about the "How" of facilitation. It is about how you show up when you step in front of a group and take on the role of facilitator. It's about *you* and who you need to be.

I cannot really teach someone how to facilitate. I can share tips, tools, and techniques, but ultimately, who you are and what you believe when you walk into the room is what will inform the impact you have as a facilitator. It is through your beliefs that your actions and words will flow.

Sometimes, when a facilitator's actions and words contradict what they want the group to do, the group will let them know right then and there. But other groups will walk out of the room and begin feeding the negative, subterranean culture of grievances that are not allowed to be spoken out loud and are instead talked about "offline." That's why understanding who you are and what you believe when you walk into the room is so critical. And that's why the focus here is on helping you develop your self-awareness and your ability to discern your impact as a group's facilitator.

This book is designed to help you stand tall in your facilitation stance—to know who you are and how you need to show up in the room, each and every time.

THE AGILE TEAM FACILITATION STANCE: FIVE GUIDING PRINCIPLES

No matter the structure of the organization, the way we work today requires some level of collaboration within teams and/or between teams, customers, and stakeholders.

Collaboration is when two or more people come together to co-create something. When collaboration is effective, it can produce a euphoric feeling of accomplishment, success, trust, and teamwork. When collaboration is ineffective, it can drain a team, creating that familiar feeling of "here we go again...same discussion, same outcome, different day." Effective or ineffective, collaboration is a messy process. You can't predict how it will go, and things don't always unfold the way you think they will. Collaboration is fundamentally emergent.

This is why facilitation is a core competency for agile coaches and why it is crucial in any organizational setting: teams need facilitators who can foster effective collaboration, support meaningful dialogue, and enable team decision-making.

Here are some common behaviors that get in the way of effective collaboration:

- *Asking for input when you've already made up your mind about what the decision or outcome will be*
- *Using your position of authority when leading a meeting to drive your own agenda and influence a particular outcome*

❖ *Expressing an unclear purpose and/or desired outcome for the collaboration*

❖ *Failing to clarify how the final decision will be made (e.g., is the group making a recommendation or a final decision? Will majority rule or will it require consensus?*

As a facilitator, if you fall into the trap of any one of these behaviors, the collaboration will be frustrating and less impactful than you might desire.

> When you are facilitating, collaboration begins with you.

Facilitation is like a complex dance of polarities. When teams come together to collaborate, topics and decisions are rarely black and white with a clear "right" answer. At any given time, when you are leading a group from a facilitative stance, you are interweaving different ideas and perspectives, creating a rich and textured network of ideas that serve to deepen understanding and seek diversity. You are helping the group define the shades of gray so that they can make more informed decisions.

It takes a high degree of self-awareness, self-management, group awareness, and group process to navigate the dance. People are putting their trust in you to lead them through a complex process. They hope to be heard, respected, and valued, and to be able to contribute to something greater than what they could accomplish on their own.

To prepare for this kind of work, facilitators must remember one fundamental rule at all times:

> You are managing yourself.

This book is structured around what I call the five guiding principles of the Agile Team Facilitation Stance. These principles provide a foundation to help facilitators support groups in doing their best work, and they offer a framework for facilitators to take a stand in themselves while promoting effective collaboration in group settings. These principles sit underneath the core facilitation skills of self-awareness, self-management, group awareness and group process.

Holding the Group's Agenda

Honoring the Wisdom of the Group

SELF-AWARENESS
SELF-MANAGEMENT
GROUP AWARENESS
GROUP PROCESS

Standing in the Storm

Upholding the Agile Mindset and Principles

Maintaining Neutrality

Principle 1: Maintaining Neutrality

At the most basic level, this principle is about you owning the process of the meeting while the team owns the content.

In practice, this principle looks like:

- *Setting the group's direction toward an agreed-upon outcome*
- *Making process moves about how the group will work*
- *Staying completely out of the topic being discussed*
- *Asking questions of the group*

+ *Bridging competing ideas*
+ *Sharing what you see in the process with facts—and without judgement*

The hardest part about neutrality is letting go of the need to share your opinion or point of view regarding the subject being discussed. For agile team facilitators or agile coaches, in particular, this can be the toughest part of the whole process, as you are often part of the team in some way, as well. You likely have knowledge about the subject the team is discussing, but must remain neutral when you hold the stance of facilitator.

In Chapter 1, I will help you deepen your awareness and knowledge around the skills of facilitation to help make it much easier to find and maintain your neutrality.

Principle 2: Standing in the Storm

This principle is about seeking out and really listening to differing points of view, perspectives, options, solutions, and paths. While the "storm" might look, feel, and behave differently with each team, this principle is about being able to recognize the storm and understanding how to weather it. It is about staying with conflict or differing opinions rather than deflecting, changing the subject, or moving on to something new.

Most groups do not naturally want to stay in conflict; they have patterns of avoiding it, often at all costs. Without taking sides, a facilitator holds the space for all to speak and be heard during a meeting. The belief here is that different points of view provide clarity, discernment, deeper understanding, and energy. Without these things, the collaboration will be less effective.

Chapter 2 addresses how to help a group stay with difference rather than avoid it—because there is greater clarity in thinking and new ideas on the other side.

Principle 3: Honoring the Wisdom of the Group

This principle, at its core, is about trust: trusting that the group has its own wisdom and everything else it needs in order to be creative and innovative in solving its own problems. The group members just need the space to access what they need.

This chapter focuses on creating a space that values the voice of each person. Everyone on the team has both wisdom to learn and wisdom to share. This principle is about believing that when each person is able to authentically voice what they see, how they think, and their own unique perspective—and that when they have an equal ability to truly listen—a group will gain access to their collective wisdom. When you trust in the collective wisdom, there is inclusiveness, less need to control what people say, and less fear that someone will "derail" the thinking. Instead, the diversity of perspectives represented by different voices will enable the group to innovate and move forward.

Rather than leaving the wisdom of the group untapped, Chapter 3 helps you create an environment where each member of the team can grow, stretch, and achieve as a respected and valued collaborator.

Principle 4: Holding the Group's Agenda

This principle is about continually asking, "How can I best serve the group?" It is about wondering, "What does this group really need right now?"

If you are facilitating a group, there will always be a meeting agenda. This is called the "presenting agenda." The presenting agenda is where the group is going and what they ultimately need. However, moving forward might require tackling the things that generally tend to be "undiscussable" in the group, and which often come up in meetings as the "emergent agenda."

Have you ever worked with a group and gotten the feeling that its members are resisting the decision that they are narrowing down toward? When every attempt to move the group forward to the next agenda item in the process is met with reluctance? This is the moment when you need to decide if you're going to stick to the "presenting agenda"—what's *supposed* to be happening in this meeting—or take a pause and edge into the "emerging agenda" of what's going on in the group. As a facilitator, understanding your choices when you encounter this moment in the room is what it means to hold the group's agenda over your own.

By addressing when and how to hold the group's agenda, Chapter 4 helps you meet whatever feelings come up (for you and for the group) with curiosity and focus.

Principle 5: Upholding the Agile Mindset

Agile facilitators and coaches have deep expertise in the practice of agility itself: the values, mindset, and practices that allow teams to adapt and change as they evolve.

Chapter 5 of this book introduces strategies to help facilitators guide a team in ways that uphold the agile values and principles in a way that works for them. This is the essence of what "agile facilitation" is all about.

When tackling each of these five principles independently, as this book does, we're pulling them apart in a way that creates a bit of an artificial construct. In reality, these principles collectively and simultaneously form the basis of your thinking when you work with groups. They inform your belief system. At any moment in time, you will likely be dancing between the different principles, weaving them together like a tapestry. You will never really let any of them fall away.

By introducing these five principles of the Agile Team Facilitation Stance, this book is intended to be a guide. It is intended to get you started on your journey and to offer a different perspective on facilitation by diving into core beliefs about who you need to be in the room. In the pages to come, I offer real-life stories about putting these principles into practice, and you will find guides in each chapter to get you started in tangible ways.

I look forward to joining you for this journey.

Whenever you reach a moment where you
are lost and don't know what to do:
Pause. Plant your feet firmly on the ground. Take a deep breath.

Stand with the principles of the facilitation stance.

Remember, whatever is happening is not really about you.
It's about them.

Slow down the pace for yourself.
Slow down what's happening in the group.

You might say, in a really slow and deliberate manner,
"Can I ask you a question? What's happening right now?"

Gather some data about what's happen-
ing for the group, from the group.

Decide what's needed next.
You don't have to figure out the next four
moves, just the one for this moment.

A BRIEF CALL TO ACTION
for New Facilitators

In general, we don't collaborate well in organizations. What does collaboration even mean? I find that people use the word in any number of different ways. Yet most leaders would probably acknowledge that, in some way, they want a collaborative environment. They want people to enjoy their work, work well with their team members, and be productive and efficient.

The promise of collaboration is that it brings "buy-in" and support, it helps us identify gaps or ideas that we might be missing, and it fosters a shared understanding about the work we will accomplish. Collaboration promises greater alignment in how we work together, enabling more autonomy in how the work gets done and making the process more enjoyable and rewarding for everyone.

That's a lot of promises.

Unfortunately, what I observe in day-to-day workplace behavior—in teams and in leadership—is that we often don't live up to the promise of collaborative thinking, collaborative work, and collaborative space.

I have written this book because I believe that facilitation is one of the foundational ways to create truly collaborative cultures, cultivate agility, improve communication, and foster shared vision and alignment. It allows for decisions to be made at the lowest possible level of the organization and creates higher autonomy and self-organization in the execution of a team's strategy and plan.

However, facilitation is possibly one of the most undervalued leadership competencies that exists. Done well, you don't really know that it's happening. To the untrained eye, it just seems like the group is high-performing. Done poorly, people often blame the leader, each other, or the norms within their organization for the experience of ineffective and unproductive meetings.

Because of its relative invisibility, facilitation, as a competency or role, is often not seen as something worth investing in. There is a general feeling that facilitation is something everyone knows how to do. But I would say that while everyone might *think* they know how to run a meeting—create an agenda, send out the meeting invite, order refreshments, prepare materials, hold the meeting, manage the time, track action items, and take notes— in reality, there is *so much more* to setting the stage for collaborative work to unfold and for effective outcomes to be achieved.

When facilitation is not recognized and valued as a specific set of skills and competencies, here's what can happen in meetings:

- *People cut each other off in mid-sentence, resulting in unwillingness to contribute to the conversation*
- *Groups keep revisiting the same decision over and over again, resulting in frustration and a lack of willingness to even attend meetings*
- *Meetings become free-for-alls with multiple people talking over one another, resulting in no real progress being made and a general sense of apathy about collaboration*
- *People start to believe that it is much more productive for someone to just make the decision without asking for input*

Because it shapes how we come together and work, facilitation is the key to collaboration. It is a competency that deserves just as much attention as the competency of leadership. When you step up to facilitate, you are filling a vital role.

FACILITATION VS. TEAM COACHING? WHAT AM I DOING AND WHY DOES IT MATTER?

If you work with agile teams, you might find yourself wondering about some key terminology along the way. What's the difference between a facilitator and a team coach, anyway? And, just as importantly, why does this distinction matter? Depending on your organization, your industry, your role, etc., these questions might feel more or less pressing.

In this section, I'll introduce some of the key distinctions, but here's the thing: **regardless of the role you play in your organization, the competencies of facilitation will help you in your practice of leading collaboration.**

Facilitation

Facilitation encompasses two different levels of focus and attention. In *The Skilled Facilitator*, Roger Schwarz offers a useful distinction between "basic facilitation" and "developmental facilitation."[2] In *basic facilitation*, the facilitator's focus primarily stays on the process and the purpose of a meeting. Usually, this means they are present to help the group solve a content problem in the moment, like how to prioritize the next two weeks of work. By contrast, *developmental facilitation* is where the facilitator focuses on improving the group process and/or dynamic in general so that there is reduced dependence on a facilitator as the conversation moves forward.

Let's dig a bit deeper. With *basic facilitation*, the facilitator helps the group focus productively on the issue at hand (the content). The facilitator is keenly aware of the content being discussed,

---

2   Roger Schwarz, *The Skilled Facilitator: A Comprehensive Resource for Consultants, Facilitators, Managers, Trainers, and Coaches* (San Francisco: Jossey-Bass, 2002), 50–51.

but they maintain their neutrality around it so that they can help the group have a meaningful conversation.

Basic
Facilitator Focus

With *developmental facilitation*, a facilitator broadens their view to encompass the group structure and communication patterns. They focus on being able to see, name, and work with the group's structural dynamics, adjusting the facilitation process as needed in order to help the group achieve their desired outcome more effectively.

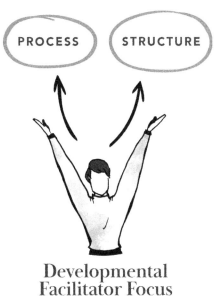

Developmental
Facilitator Focus

Team coaching

With *team coaching*, the focus shifts again. A team coach's *primary* focus is on the group dynamics and structure. They help a group see and make sense of their dynamics in order to improve as a team and change the nature of their outcomes. The coach enables the team to nurture more awareness so that they can make intentional choices about what processes they use and what they can achieve together.

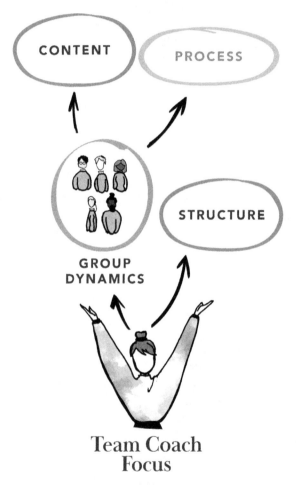

**Team Coach
Focus**

At the point when you are knee-deep in the process of developmental facilitation, you will start to notice that there is a fine line between the competencies of group facilitation and team coaching. In fact, developmental facilitation acts as a sort of bridge between basic facilitation and team coaching. Although team coaching is a different skill set than facilitation and requires additional competencies, *all* of the facilitation skills and competencies are necessary and valuable when you take on this role.

One of the most important distinctions between facilitation and team coaching is that the group grants the facilitator much more power in the meeting room than they would a team coach. Facilitation has more process authority (process "leadership," if you like) because the facilitator is directing and guiding the process in the room toward a specific, desired outcome. In this scenario, the facilitator helps the group focus closely on the conversation (the content). As you can see, the same skills will be useful for team coaching, even though a team coach's focus in the room is a bit different.

	BASIC FACILITATION	DEVELOPMENTAL FACILITATION	TEAM COACHING
Purpose	Lead the meeting process.	Empower the team to facilitate themselves.	Empower the team to lead and tackle more systemic challenges.
Focus	Group process for achieving tasks and outcomes. Focus is on making meetings run better and more collaboratively.	How the group is working. Focus is on improving team interactions, communications, and decision-making skills.	How the system is working. Focus is on the system as a whole and how it's working or not working.

	BASIC FACILITATION	DEVELOPMENTAL FACILITATION	TEAM COACHING
Symptoms	Team needs help with meetings.	Challenges with behavior or interpersonal relationships.	Systemic challenges and stuck patterns that are keeping the team from their full potential.
Sounds like	"Help us get better at running our release planning meetings."	"Help us improve how we work so we can facilitate our own work."	"Help us develop as a team so that we can reach high performance."
Leadership	Active leadership from the facilitator, who takes the "process lead" by designing a process to help the group achieve their desired outcomes.	Active leadership from the facilitator, but leadership happens more from the back than the front. The emphasis is on building the team's capacity to be more self-facilitating and self-organizing.	Active leadership is happening within the team itself. The team is doing their real work either in a meeting, in a work session, or at their desks while the coach observes and intervenes when appropriate or needed.
Outcomes	Achievement of a specific goal or deliverable (e.g., team charter, decision on work priorities, release plan, etc.).	Improvements in awareness, skills, and effectiveness as a team.	Positive changes in individual and team performance. Individual and group shifts in mindset, deepened awareness and intentionality about working together effectively.

	BASIC FACILITATION	DEVELOPMENTAL FACILITATION	TEAM COACHING
What are you doing?	Creating a clear meeting purpose, agenda, working agreements, and a process that engages the whole group. Helping the team learn the agile practices, including stand-up, team chartering, iteration planning, release planning, and retrospective.	Naming structural patterns so the group can become more aware of their helpful vs. unhelpful patterns. Designing group processes to help change the patterns observed in the team.	Live and "in the moment" coaching opportunities with the team, including neutrally naming what is happening so that the team can see it and take their own actions.
How are difficult problems handled?	Mostly "off-line" or one-toone, and including feedback about impact.	Challenging patterns in the group by naming them, then helping group members navigate the challenges or developing working agreements to prevent them.	Problems are seen as systemic issues rather than one-to-one conversations. They are worked on with the whole system in the room. "Bring the conversation in the room" is a guiding principle.
What level of self-mastery might be needed here?	Awareness of your own behavioral profile and how it might impact the team.	Increasing awareness and ability to see patterns in the moment— yours and others. Expanding your tolerance for difference. Becoming "multi-lingual" (i.e., able to change your vocal range when needed).	Changing your behavior in order to help the team change their pattern and get different results.

On your journey to masterful facilitation, you are likely to encounter tension and even confusion around the distinctions between facilitation and team coaching. To make matters harder, the terms sometimes get used interchangeably. So, when you're working with a team, you don't necessarily need to teach them these definitions. But you *do* need to clearly discern what stance or role you are inhabiting at any given time. This is because these roles each require a slightly different container and designed alliance with the team. They also require different mindsets, competencies, and presence from you as the practitioner. You need to be clear about what role you are in and feel able to communicate what you're doing in language that the team will understand.

Let's imagine what this would look like in the real world. Imagine you are working with a group as a facilitator and you notice the group has become stuck in a conversation. Your efforts to shake it up (moving them around the room, asking them to write on stickies, etc.) are just not working. Reading the room, you realize that the thing holding the group back might not be the thing they are discussing at all. It might be time to delve into developmental facilitation or even put your team coach hat on. If you do, it's time to communicate clearly with the group and let them join you in designing the next steps.

If you're pivoting between roles like this, here's what it might sound like when you communicate your observations and actions to the team:

> "Let's pause for a moment. I'm noticing that you seem to be going in circles and not getting anywhere. We are only hearing from three people and others have become silent. I've been holding the role of facilitator today and focusing on the process to help you achieve your desired purpose. But my sense is that there is more here to talk about. I

would like to suggest we suspend the outcome for today and instead turn our focus to the group dynamics so that you can explore how to change them for yourselves. How does this sound?"

When you have clarity around your role, you will know what you're doing and why you're doing it, which will help you be more effective when you are designing a group process with the team. Without this clarity, you risk (at best) the team feeling confused about what you're trying to do. At worst, you risk that your good intentions in the room will have a very negative impact on the team as a whole or on specific individuals. People might feel exposed, called out, or stepped on, which results in distrust of you as a practitioner.

At the most basic level, your ability to discern and navigate the primary components of facilitation and coaching will strengthen the skill set you bring to your work.

STRIKING THE BALANCE

A final word as you begin this next phase of your facilitation journey: **beware of either/or thinking**.

When you start to deepen your facilitation skills and experience, you will likely encounter gremlins along the way. These negative voices might come from your own thinking, or they might come from teams or leaders that you contract with. But regardless of the origin, it will help to remember one key fact: to effectively facilitate, you must learn to sit in the uncomfortable space of *polarity*—which means being able to hold the tension of what feels like opposing viewpoints.

Your success as a facilitator will be informed by how well you grow your ability to hold complex subjects that feel at odds with one another—to work with both of them and to help others do the same. So, before launching into the thick of the facilitation stance, I want to introduce you to some common assumptions you are likely to meet in order to help you steer clear of this either/or thinking.

Polarity 1: Efficiency vs. Collaboration

The assumption: we can either get something done quickly OR we can come to consensus about an idea.

This either/or polarity is premised on the belief that collaboration is not efficient. And sure, collaboration does take time. But where might you lose efficiency further down the road if people are not in alignment about the work being done now, or if they don't fully understand the thought process behind the decision being made? I recently decided to take a more "efficient" route in my business by skipping a longer, more collaborative process. As I look back on that decision, it has not saved me any time or resources. Quite frankly, it will end up being more costly as we backtrack and bring those who were left confused by the new direction back into the process.

How often do you spend time in unproductive conversations, or with team members who are not able to contribute effectively because they don't fully understand why certain things are being done or how specific topics became the priority? The cost of ineffective work has an impact on time and money, but it also has a high impact on morale. People *want* to be contributing members of high-performing teams.

Simply telling someone what to do does not make a process more effective. Conversations and meaning-making is the work to do.

So, what happens if we believe in both collaboration *and* efficiency? That collaboration can, in fact, *lead* to efficiency? It might not feel efficient in the moment, but collaboration fosters efficiency over time in the form of fewer mistakes, fewer misunderstandings in communication and execution, and greater understanding of interdependencies.

Polarity 2: Maintaining neutrality vs. Having a point of view

The assumption: I can either have a point of view OR maintain neutrality.

The idea here is that you can't do both; it's just too hard. Or that if you are facilitating, you are overstepping your bounds if you have your own perspective.

Being neutral can take practice, which we'll discuss at length in Chapter 1. What I want you to take away here is that maintaining neutrality and having a point of view do not have to be at odds with one another. Both can be true.

I will often have a point of view about the content of a conversation I'm facilitating. The key (what makes it more palatable for the group) is the *way* that point of view is offered when we are facilitating. When it's stated like a fact—like you are right and the group is wrong—then it does not feel great to the group. However, when your point of view is stated and used with permission from the group, it can be productive. For example, if I see a group stuck on prioritization and resisting the budget that's been set, I won't just jump in to correct them with a statement like, "No, you can't do that, you don't have enough money." Instead, I will say something like, "The budget is tight, and I'm noticing the group is selecting items that are more costly compared to other options. What's another way you could look at your selection criteria?"

Instead of fixing the situation or correcting the group, your role is to help them find a different doorway or perspective to explore in their conversation.

In fact, when facilitation is done well—when it's active and engaged—it brings its own point of view about the group process (i.e., team effectiveness, collaboration, decision-making, clarity of roles and responsibilities, and expertise in effective communication and conflict). And this point of view about process means actively engaging and helping a group navigate all facets of their work together. If you're doing this well, you likely won't even have much head space to devote to the content.

Neutrality does not mean silence or passivity. You will absolutely have points of view. Use your perspective and opinion to help you frame genuinely curious questions that foster new thinking for the group.

Polarity 3: Holding *my* agenda (having a stake in the outcome) vs. Holding the *group's* agenda

> The assumption: I can either have a stake in the outcome OR I can hold the group's agenda. I can't do both.

If you are wearing multiple hats, meaning you are facilitating but also holding a role like leader, manager, key decision-maker,

Scrum master, or agile coach, etc., you will likely encounter this particular polarity. It's tricky! And it takes experience to navigate. You will need to hold onto the belief that learning in the team *will* result in missteps or "getting it wrong." You will have to consider when it's worth the learning opportunity and when you actually *do* need to step in and override what the team is doing. Just know that every time you override the team, you are subtly disempowering them and sending the message that they can't do it. That failure is not an option. That it's not safe to fail here.

Being held accountable and responsible for the team's performance while letting them make the decisions (holding their agenda) is possible if you believe that the wisdom is there. In fact, your agenda is probably not that far off from the team's agenda, it's just that the road they take might look different than yours. Whether to hold their agenda will be your call to make in the moment. When are you willing to learn together and see what unfolds, and when do you need to step forward and make a clear decision?

You can hold the perceived polarity of the group's agenda versus your own—and avoid either/or thinking about it—by being honest and transparent with yourself and the group about where you have bias and where you would like their input. Don't ask for input from the team if you are just going to overrule them. If you know there is a chance of that happening, tell them up front. No one wants to show up for an hour-long meeting, get invested in a topic they care about, and spend the time coming to a decision only to have it undone by someone else after the meeting has concluded.

And if you are the ultimate decision-maker and you are leaning one way or the other, tell the group where you are leaning. Be clear about how you will make the decision, and be clear about what aspects you want to open up to the group. There is no need for either/or thinking here unless there is a lack of communication.

As you set forth on your facilitation journey, it's good to be aware of where you might run into hiccups. Whether it comes from the struggle to maintain clarity around your role in the room or falling into the trap of either/or thinking, there are times when you will know you could have done it differently. But that's what this book is here for. Together, we'll walk through the five principles of your facilitation stance and arm you with practices to use within and beyond the meeting room.

It takes practice, but you got this!

CHAPTER 1:

Maintaining Neutrality

In simplest terms, the role of a facilitator in a collaborative meeting is to bring an objective and unbiased view to a group process so that all voices can be heard and the team can access its collective intelligence. One of the best ways to achieve this is for a facilitator to maintain neutrality. How? By owning the *process* of the meeting while letting the participants own the content or topic.

Owning the process of the meeting means you will engage in the following actions:

- *Setting the group's direction toward an agreed-upon outcome*
- *Making process moves about how the group will work*
- *Staying completely out of the topic being discussed*
- *Asking questions of the group*
- *Building bridges between competing ideas*
- *Sharing what you see happening in the group's process without judgement*

That sounds easy, doesn't it? In theory, it is easy. It's dead simple.

In practice? No. Not easy. In fact, some would argue that being completely neutral is not possible, that everything we say and do will be informed by our bias. While I don't entirely disagree with that idea, I *do* think it's possible to maintain neutrality—especially if your focus is on the process and not the content.

Owning the process of a meeting means letting go of your need to share your opinion or point of view on the topic being discussed. Especially if you are a part of the team in some way, as agile team facilitators and agile coaches are, this can be a very tough part of the process. But when you hold the stance of facilitator, this is your role. Remaining neutral builds greater trust within the team and allows you to see the bigger picture of what's being said (and not said) in the room. When you remain neutral, your contribution becomes more important than just asserting a point of view. It becomes about helping the group navigate the content in an effective and productive manner.

In this chapter, we will explore the difference between content and process, and we will deepen your ability to find and maintain neutrality. As a result of developing this facilitation stance, you will be able to help the groups you work with build trust and confidence in their own ability to find effective solutions.

BUILDING TRUST WITHIN THE GROUP

When you remain neutral as the facilitator, you subtly reflect to the group that they have the wisdom needed to find the right solution or path. This is about empowering the team and helping them find their way rather than disempowering them by jumping in with your own opinions.

Neutrality means remaining free from judgement about good or bad, right or wrong. There is an openness in it that makes room for more than one truth and more than one solution. With neutrality comes more trust, and with trust comes more confidence for each member in the group as a whole. As a team, trust and confidence means an ease and eagerness to continue the momentum. It means greater velocity, more effectiveness, improved solutions, and more options.

By contrast, when a facilitator offers advice or jumps into problem solving, it increases a team's dependence on them. It sends the subtle and unstated message that you don't think they're capable of doing the work. Over time, the action of leaping into "answer mode" undermines the team's confidence and their ability to access and voice their collective intelligence.

Neutrality offers the gift of "not knowing," of being able to take a different perspective. It allows you to see another way and to dance in the space of exploration. Fully standing in the space of neutrality says to a group, "I'm your sherpa. I'll guide you up this mountain. There is a specific process we will follow, but, in the end, you'll know that you can do the work."

Yet no matter how much you believe in the power of collective intelligence and the importance of creating an environment where it can flourish, maintaining neutrality is a difficult practice. It can be very difficult to actively achieve and maintain during the course of a meeting, especially when the person in the facilitator role has an opinion on the topic or content being discussed. If you're an agile facilitator, in particular, it can sometimes feel downright impossible. You're a part of the team! You've just stepped into the role of facilitator to help guide the group through practices like team start-up, retrospectives, release planning, iteration planning, etc. You will likely have an opinion or even a stake in the outcome—and you might be very tempted to state it.

But maintaining neutrality is worth it. You are a part of the team, yet you play a critical role *apart* from the team. When you acknowledge this tension and still commit to stepping into the role of content-neutral facilitator, you will be supporting your team and their growth by creating a group culture where all voices can be heard.

Right now, you may not be entirely sure if you can maintain neutrality in your group. But, given the payoff, that shouldn't stop you from trying.

HOLD THE PROCESS, NOT THE CONTENT

The first time I facilitated a group of 25 people, I was scared to death. My fears were about wanting to be prepared, wanting the meeting to go well, wanting to provide value, and wanting to show my expertise. I spent quite a bit of my preparation time mapping out a detailed plan, making a back-up plan for every possible event, and doing my homework on the topic so I was knowledgeable about some of the issues that might come up as questions. I wanted to have an *answer*.

At the time, having *the answer* felt important because I wanted to prove my credibility by ensuring that my facilitation would increase the group's productivity. What you might be noticing is that the theme of all my fears and the focus of all my preparation was, ultimately, *me*. And by letting my fears get a foot in the door, I risked letting *my* preconceived ideas about what *I* thought constituted a "win" for the group guide my process in the room. This is not unusual for new facilitators. Even after practicing facilitation for 25 years, there are still times when I want to be fully in the content and have someone *else* hold the process.

Honoring the importance of neutrality is the first step to developing true facilitation skills and cultivating successful group collaboration.

A facilitator's domain is presence and awareness for the way the group is proceeding through the agenda or the problem at hand. **This is the *process*.** It is not about trying to provide answers regarding the topic on the table or subtly guiding the group in one direction or another in relation to it. **That is the *content*.** Understanding the difference between the *process* and the *content* is key for becoming a skillful facilitator—you have to be able to monitor yourself and ensure you are not crossing from one to the other, even when you want to.

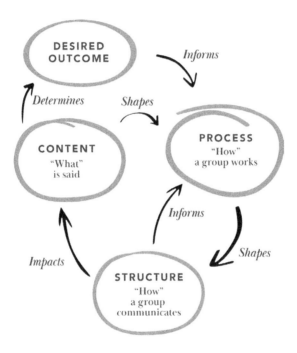

Without a lens for separating content and process, we compound them together. So, the first skill in facilitation is separating the WHAT from the HOW. The "what" is the subject of the conversation—the **content**. The "how" includes both the group's **process** (how the group works) and, drawing from David Kantor's research on group communication, the group's **structure** (how the group communicates).

CONTENT "WHAT" IS BEING SAID The subject of the conversation	GROUP PROCESS "HOW" A GROUP WORKS Places to intervene and shift, changing the nature of the outcome by focusing on the behavior and conversational structure

• The purpose
• The desired outcome
• The meeting agenda
• The subject or topics of conversation
• The actions
• The decisions
	• The space
	  ◦ Room design and setup (virtual or in person)
	• The group dynamics
	  ◦ The group membership
	  ◦ Who is in the room
	  ◦ The power dynamics
	  ◦ The relationships
	  ◦ The energy
	  ◦ The group or team
	• The container
	  ◦ Creating connections
	  ◦ Intention setting
	  ◦ Roles, responsibilities, and authority
	  ◦ Accountability
	  ◦ Working agreements
	  ◦ Group norms
	  ◦ Feedback
	  ◦ Decision-making agreements
	• Collaboration processes
	  ◦ Exploring ideas
	  ◦ Evaluating alternatives
	  ◦ Deciding
	  ◦ Working with conflict

STRUCTURE
"HOW" A GROUP COMMUNICATES
The structure of face to face communication

• The words used
• The manner in which words are said
• The intention behind how words are said
• The impact of how words are said
• The sequence, flow, and structure of the vocal actions
• The conversation

Even when you're able to separate these components, however, you'll probably still notice how easy it is within group settings for a facilitator—especially if they are also a leader within the group—to get caught up in offering solutions to the content being presented. It can feel very difficult to just stay curious and ask questions of the group instead.

Why is this?

It starts with a myth—a myth based in fear—that many leaders and facilitators believe in. The myth is that they must contribute verbally or share their opinions and suggestions in order to be perceived as contributing value in their position. Discomfort around neutrality can actually (and easily) be compounded by the culture of an organization and how people are rewarded in it.

Because the idea of neutrality gets right at the heart of how we traditionally feel we add value in conversations, this guiding principle is where I notice the most immediate resistance and pushback among the many leaders, facilitators, and coaches I work with.

The belief that verbalized opinions and contributions add more value is simply not true. In fact, when we believe that our value stems from our ability to make the right suggestion or "see the right solution" better than the group, we are actually equating *neutrality* with *passivity*.

The work of a facilitator or facilitative leader is far from passive. But the action looks different. The active attention of a facilitator is on asking questions and trusting the group to provide answers. As a facilitator, you watch for hidden dynamics in the group. You focus on inquiring, staying with curiosity, and inviting participants to dig deeper within themselves for more insight and new understanding. Teams can be greatly influenced by a slight comment or when too much attention is paid to one idea or another. This susceptibility makes it even more important for a facilitator to be constantly and actively monitoring themselves. When you are trying to pay attention to the content, there is a danger that you're missing what's happening inside the process.

FIELD MAINTENANCE

Imagine that a facilitator has just taken the group through an exercise. There are large sheets scribed with details and feedback hanging on the wall. Everyone takes a breath to review all the content that has emerged from the exercise.

A new facilitator's immediate instinct may be to summarize what she sees. She might even say something like, "Looks like we have a winner here!" But if she does, she is crossing from the space of *process* and into the territory of *content*. This is because, no matter how well intentioned, her action has come from a place of **knowing** instead of a place of **inquiry**. Remember: what the facilitator sees from her place in the room will be different from what the group sees. And the group will *always* know more about the intention and meaning behind the words that they created than the facilitator will.

Your role as a facilitator is to help the conversation unfold. Each step in the process opens a doorway into a different level of the discussion. If you jump ahead and draw a conclusion for the group, you are missing out on helping them come to a deeper level of shared understanding around the content. This matters, because when a group deepens their understanding, they will find more clarity and refinement in their thinking, and they will be able to find new ideas that will bring them closer to collective alignment around the next step the group should take.

Is the action of summarization helpful? Perhaps—as a content owner. But the facilitator is the **process owner.**

So, what could this facilitator have done instead?

A "neutral" approach would have been to ask of the group: "What do **you** see?"

This distinction is subtle, but very powerful. In your role as facilitator, it is not important what a group produces on the sheets of paper over the course of an exercise (the content). What *is* important is how the group talks about and moves forward with what they have produced (the process).

Especially if you are both a member of the team *and* the person who has stepped into the role of facilitator, remaining neutral and focusing on the process can feel like you are biting your tongue. If the team is struggling with how to move forward and you feel like you have an idea that would help, it might feel difficult not to voice it. So, as you start to develop your practice, it can be helpful to keep in mind some common phrases that indicate you are delving into content, as well as some alternatives you might consider to keep you on the process side of things.

INSTEAD OF THIS...	TRY THIS...
It sounds like we have all the ideas on the table.	We've heard from two of you. What does someone else see?
Looks like we have a decision.	I notice there are three votes for one option and one vote for the other. Would someone like to speak to the option that currently has one vote?
Here's what I see… *or,* Seems like...	What do you see?

INSTEAD OF THIS...	TRY THIS...
I think it would be helpful if...	What do you need to move forward?
Let's move on.	What are we missing? What do you need in order to move to the next step?

Remember: the value you bring is in owning the process and in holding the space so that the group can do its best work with the content.

WHAT WE BELIEVE MATTERS

Maintaining neutrality is about putting your own ego aside. As we've seen, it's easy to fall into the trap of believing that the only way to provide value to a team is to problem solve for them. But this is not the case. A facilitator's value stems from helping teams problem solve *for themselves*.

When you step into the role of facilitating a team, it is of utmost importance to cultivate the tools you need to maintain neutrality. And the number one tool you have at your fingertips is *yourself and your beliefs*:

* *What you believe about yourself*
* *What you believe about the group*
* *What you believe about the value of facilitation*

So, before you even set foot in the room, it's crucial to understand the link between internal beliefs and the actions you are equipped (or not) to take in the role of facilitator.

46

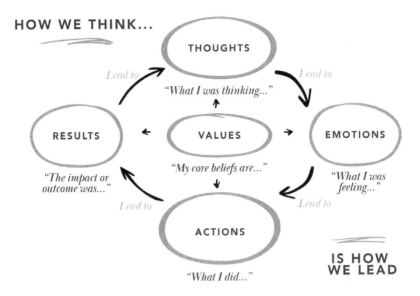

HOW WE THINK...

THOUGHTS

Lead to ... *Lead to*

"*What I was thinking...*"

RESULTS — VALUES → EMOTIONS

"*The impact or outcome was...*" "*My core beliefs are...*" "*What I was feeling...*"

Lead to ... *Lead to*

ACTIONS

"*What I did...*"

IS HOW WE LEAD

How we think is how we act and how we lead.

The models dictating how we personally engage—how we communicate and interact with others—get laid down very early on in our lives. David Kantor calls these "childhood stories," and suggests that they emerge during early childhood and into adolescence (from about 2 years old through 22 years old).[3] The way we interact with others in these early years creates structural patterns ("stories") that guide how we behave when we encounter similar structures in the future.

The stories of our childhood form our beliefs and values (what we hold to be important about how we engage with others). These beliefs are often formed in relation to how we want to feel in the moment, and they ultimately lead to our actions (the things we say or do in the moment). In turn, our actions have an impact on others, and that impact (the result of our actions) informs our stories and beliefs. When the results of our actions don't align with our beliefs or they don't make us feel how we want to feel in

---

3   David Kantor, *Reading the Room: Group Dynamics for Coaches and Leaders* (San Francisco: Jossey-Bass, 2012).

the moment, we might begin to feel *dissonance*. When the results of our actions and the impact they have aligns with our beliefs and feelings, we will likely feel more *resonance*.

So, what in the world does all this have to do with facilitation? Quite simply, it suggests that what you believe about yourself, about groups, and about communication will closely inform the actions you take, the impact you have, and the results the group is able to achieve.[4]

Our first work in facilitation is therefore self-awareness. What I offer here is a way to help you look at your own beliefs in order to help you become more aware of how you lead and why you do what you do.

Let's look at how some of our internal beliefs and assumptions about facilitation and neutrality might show up as practices in the room.

NEUTRAL (I.E., OWNING THE PROCESS)

Internal assumptions and beliefs

- I am active and engaged (not passive)
- I own the process, the group owns the content
- I add value by reflecting back to the group what's actually happening
- I am open minded and see value in all voices
- Polarities in opinions offer opportunities to find common ground
- I am vested in helping the group achieve their desired outcomes
- Critique about the group process is not a critique about who I am

---

4   For further reading, see: Chris Argysis, "Double Loop Learning in Organizations," *Harvard Business Review* (September 1977); Carol Dweck, *Mindset: The Psychology of Success* (Random House, 2006); and Kantor, *Reading the Room.*

NEUTRAL (I.E., OWNING THE PROCESS)

Practices in the room

- I say what I see in a factual, non-judgmental way ("I'm noticing...")
- I take a systems perspective
- I bridge competing ideas
- I listen for the 2% common ground
- I offer ideas with no attachment to the outcome
- I inquire by asking powerful questions
- I seek to understand and deepen the group's understanding

NOT NEUTRAL (I.E., DRIVING THE CONTENT)

Internal assumptions and beliefs

- I am valuable because of my superior capability, experience, knowledge, or insight
- The group will make the wrong decision if I don't add my experience
- If I left it to the group, we would never be done
- I have too much at stake to facilitate without bias
- My value is determined by my ability to add value to these discussions
- Neutrality means being passive, so if I can't offer my opinion, I won't say anything

Practices in the room

- I use my positional authority as meeting leader to contribute my idea
- I just make decisions for the sake of time management
- I comment positively on the contributions made by some but not others
- I disregard input from those who don't align with my thinking
- I speak over people
- I am the one doing the majority of the talking
- I allow my design to reinforce biases (e.g., only hearing from those who like to talk)
- I over-contribute to the content
- I drive toward a particular outcome

As you read the list of above, you might notice yourself having the reaction of "Yes, but…" If you find a few statements from the "not neutral" examples that resonate with you, you might find maintaining neutrality difficult. You might say, "Yes, but I sometimes drop neutrality for good reasons!" You might feel like your team just does not get it and they need your help. Or, you might worry that if you were to stop adding content, the meetings would produce nothing.

If you find yourself defending reasons to drive the content, don't worry. You'll find practices in the next section to help you transition into neutrality with more comfort around these potential sticking points.

Then there's the other end of the "Yes, but…" spectrum. You might feel fully aligned with the beliefs listed under the "neutral" column, *but* you don't see how it's possible to translate these beliefs into actions or practices in the room. Here, too, the practices I introduce in the next section will help.

Neutrality is a tricky concept, even for me! No matter how informed or self-aware I might be about where I have opinions and where I don't, it's easy for me to have an "off" day. I might get hooked by the topic and find myself contributing content or voting on an outcome without realizing it. The importance of understanding how your own set of internal beliefs and stories informs your actions is that it gives you something to come back to, an anchor of self-understanding, so that you can learn to manage yourself more effectively in a role where neutrality matters to the group's outcome.

STARTING THE PRACTICE

Once you have started the hard work of aligning your internal beliefs and assumptions about yourself and about your value as a facilitator, the time has come to practice the principle of maintaining neutrality.

This will be an ongoing practice.

First, imagine you are standing in front of a new team, one you've just started working with. They are a fairly high-performing team and have some great expectations for what they want to achieve in the meeting. You've been asked to facilitate because they feel like you would help them get through a complex planning initiative across multiple disciplines.

You're excited to be here! You've been working with another team for a while, and you've been feeling good about what they have been able to accomplish through your work with them. Being asked to facilitate for this top, high-performing team therefore feels like an honor and a great next step. You don't want to screw it up.

You get the meeting started with a clear purpose and agenda, and things seem to be off to a good start. But when you get about halfway through the meeting, you notice that the team is starting to get bogged down. Three voices in particular begin to emerge with pretty entrenched perspectives, and they start to clash with another set of voices that hold a very different viewpoint.

You look at the clock. You start to feel anxious about the time, realizing that the group feels pretty far off from coming to a decision on the topic at hand. So, you decide to intervene in the hopes that if you speed up this conversation, they will be more willing to just move forward. You make a move, saying, "What if you tried Option A? It seems like the majority of folks here agree and want to move in that direction."

All of a sudden, the team turns on you. The aggravation that was being voiced between a couple of people is now trained on you, the facilitator. Suddenly, the team wants to argue with *you* about the pros and cons of the options on the table. You immediately go from feeling confident and purposeful to feeling challenged and flustered.

As this imagination exercise illuminates, it can be somewhat shocking to feel like you've been getting good results with one team, only to find yourself in a very different situation when you begin facilitating a different team. It can feel especially jarring and uncomfortable when the team you're moving into has higher stakes and a higher performance record.

While it's impossible to know for sure, chances are that if this facilitator's default was to drive content when they faced a challenge, this was probably not the first time they'd done so. Most likely, this facilitator just hadn't received (or noticed) negative feedback that they had been stepping out of the process and into the content. A great warning signal that you've strayed outside your role as a facilitator is if you feel like you have been pulled or hooked into a debate and find yourself needing to defend something.

The following lessons are about helping you prepare to stay neutral and in the *process*, whether you have been working with a team for a while or you are entering a new group environment. While there are always surprises when you facilitate group meetings, these practices will help you pivot more effectively when you encounter uncomfortable and unproductive situations.

Lesson 1: Know before you go…

In the story above, it would have been much easier for the facilitator to maintain their neutrality if they had known in advance why the team was meeting, what they hoped to accomplish, who was coming, and who needed to be in the room. This is called Planning and Design for Facilitation—and it happens before you even step foot in the room.

First, let's take a look at the facilitation process in full. As the diagram below shows, there are five steps involved in every facilitation:

- *Plan*
- *Design*
- *Conduct*
- *Document and Evaluate*
- *Adapt*

THE FACILITATION PROCESS

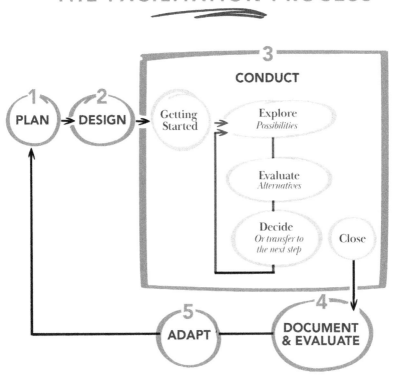

Planning and design ecompass the first two steps of any facilitation. They happen before you get started and feed directly into how you work with a group. It's the part of the process that sets you up for remaining neutral in the room—no matter what comes up as you help the group do its own work.

Planning is where you define a clear purpose and set of objectives prior to the meeting. Design sets the arc of the meeting and defines how the objectives will be reached. Together, the planning and design steps of a facilitation process ensure that you start with a clear focus and conduct a meeting that will be valuable time spent for all participants.

Here's how to do it:

- **Interview the sponsor (the person(s) who stands to gain the most from the outcome of the meeting).** *Why are they bringing the group together for a meeting? What do they hope to accomplish? What scope of authority and decision-making will the team have?*
- **Learn about the team members who will be present at the meeting.** *What concerns do they have? What do they hope to accomplish?*
- **Ask what voices, information, or data are needed in the room.** *Who and what are essential to the process? What needs to be accounted for to ensure that all the relevant pieces are in place for a productive meeting?*
- **Review the high-level design with the sponsor.** *This will prevent them from being surprised and potentially derailing the meeting once it has begun.*

A good rule of thumb here is to spend 2.5 times the length of the meeting in planning and design. Example: a 2-hour meeting = 5 hours of planning and designing the facilitation process.

And remember: especially when a key stakeholder is absent for a meeting, it can feel like you, as facilitator, are supposed to fill that role. It can feel like you need to defend why something was done or not done. **But this is not your role as a facilitator.** Going through the planning and design process will help you develop and maintain your clarity on this point.

Lesson 2: Learn a model for group dynamics

One way to stay out of the content is to focus your attention on the group dynamics.

How we communicate with one another either propels a group forward or holds it back. Models and frameworks for communication, behavior, and group dynamics help us make sense of what's happening in the room and allow us to focus on something other than our own ego or personal agenda. They help us get out of our own heads and connect with a vision that is more compelling and inspiring than self-preservation and self-protection.

Having a deep understanding of the theory and science behind group dynamics will also inform how you guide the meeting. You will be able to see more clearly which processes are likely to support a group shift that will allow them to deepen their understanding, generate new ideas, and reach clear decisions.

So, before you even enter a room, have a model or models that provide you with a basis for understanding how groups and teams interact and perform. The core model that sits under the content of this book is Structural Dynamics, encompassing David Kantor's theory of face-to-face communication.[5] This is the most impactful and morally neutral frame I've found to make sense of how groups and teams get stuck and where conflict emerges in conversation. Because they are behaviorally based, Structural Dynamics are visible in the room and, with practice, you will be able to see the structure of the interactions in groups.

Other helpful models include the Drexler/Sibbet Team Performance Model and the Diamond of Participatory Decision Making developed by Sam Kaner.[6] Whether you start with one

---

5   Kantor, *Reading the Room.*

6   For the latter, see Sam Kaner, *Facilitator's Guide to Participatory Decision-Making* (San Francisco: Jossey-Bass, 2014).

or dive into them all, using these resources to deepen your understanding of how individuals and groups tick will help you feel like a compass is guiding you each time you step into a room.

Plus, learning a model or two for group dynamics will help enormously when it comes to weathering group conflict, which is the subject of Chapter 2.

Lesson 3: Share neutral leadership

Sharing neutral leadership means sharing the work of facilitation by rotating the role among the team members. It means having everyone take a turn owning the process and stepping out of the content.

This can be a powerful practice when you are working with a team on an ongoing basis. Not only does it deepen the group's understanding of the facilitator's role and value, it helps you develop your ability to recognize what neutrality looks and feels like—and to notice when it has been lost.

To share neutral leadership, everyone in the room takes a turn as group facilitator. While in rotation, each person will notice that they need to pay attention to many different things simultaneously:

- *Individual dynamics*
- *System dynamics*
- *Interpersonal communications*
- *Who's stepping forward to participate and who's withdrawing or stepping back*
- *The difference between what's being said and what isn't*
- *The signs and indicators that there's an elephant in the room*

These are the subtle yet critical elements—the work—that a facilitator maintains in order to hold the space for their group.

When group members share in the practice of focusing on the group process and group dynamics, they will discover that there is a surprising amount of information to take in and process. They—like you—will deepen their awareness of neutrality's importance and their ability to notice when it's not being maintained.

Sharing neutral leadership is a powerful practice that simultaneously helps you develop your own skill set around maintaining neutrality and the group's ability to dig for their solutions with more trust.

Lesson 4: Ask for feedback and support

Because neutrality can be tricky, a feedback process is essential for learning what is and isn't working.

Remember that diagram of the whole Facilitation Process in Lesson 1? Well, asking for feedback and support are part of Step 4: Document and Evaluate. It's not about asking whether participants *liked* the facilitation, it's about determining if the group reached their desired outcomes through the facilitation process and if they held conversations that needed to be had. This is useful feedback for you as a facilitator, and it will likely inform the process you design for that group the next time.

We often have blind spots. Sometimes we just can't tell that we are contributing content in small, nuanced ways. Other times, we don't realize that we're defaulting to old patterns of driving content. So, the key is to find ways of asking for feedback and support that will help you grow your self-awareness and facilitation skills. This is something to do early on, when you are just starting to embrace the role of facilitator.

In my experience, co-facilitation is a great way to receive feedback, as long as you partner with someone more experienced.

Co-facilitation in this context means having someone else in the room who can see where you might have slipped out of neutrality and can help you reflect on why it happened.

You can also receive feedback directly from your team. After the meeting, ask your team about the impact the meeting had on them individually and on their overall objectives. You can ask them to write the answers to these questions on a card as they are leaving the room or create a quick web-based survey after the session.

Here is a detailed breakdown of the kinds of questions you could ask:

Process	◆ Did we use our time effectively?
	◆ How included did you feel in the process?
	◆ To what extent do you feel you were able to voice your perspective?
	◆ How well did we do on making sure everyone was involved?
	◆ Overall, how well was the meeting run?
Objectives	◆ Did we achieve what we needed to?
	◆ If not, did we accomplish something else just as meaningful or needed?
	◆ How well did we stay focused on the purpose?
Topic/Content	◆ Did we talk about the right things?
	◆ Are we using our time effectively?
	◆ Is there anything that needs to be talked about that we are missing?
Decision(s) made	◆ Asking for feedback about the decisions is not recommended and runs the risk of opening back up the work you did in the meeting to narrow down options and come to a decision. So generally it's best to stay away from this topic. If you feel a need for feedback here, you might ask if the decision is clear or actionable, but don't ask if people like or agree with it— that's the work done in the meeting.

Room setup/ configuration	◆ How did the room setup (in person or online) support or detract from collaboration?

The experience	◆ If you're curious about the overall process, ask participants for **Impact Feedback:**[7]
	  ◆ What was I doing and what was the impact on you?
	  ◆ What would have made it different or better?

A word of caution about feedback: everyone will have some.

Asking people for happy/sad stickers at the end of a meeting is a reactionary level of feedback and has very little use in growing your facilitation skills or helping you adapt and learn.[8] At best, it's a "did everyone like me or this process" kind of assessment. This is not a helpful lens. Your goal is to help a team see how they're working together and to make interventions to help change the nature of group patterns. This can and will make many people uncomfortable, and they may not like it—or you—in the process. The impact, over time, can be invaluable to the group, but reactionary feedback will not help you get there any faster.

Once you have collected *useful* feedback, you have the opportunity to **adapt your process** (the final stage of the Facilitation Process diagram introduced earlier). Adapting is your opportunity to continuously improve your processes. Take care to allow for your own learning and give yourself space and time

---

7   This term comes from a model for feedback called the Situation – Behavior – Impact™ (SBI™) Feedback Tool, which was developed by the Center for Creative Leadership. You can find more information in their "Feedback that Works" program: https://www.mindtools.com/pages/article/situation-behavior-impact-feedback.htm

8   See James D. and Wendy Kayser Kirkpatrick, *Four Levels of Training Evaluation* (Alexandria: ATD Press, 2016).

to collect data over several meetings and to really reflect on it before making major changes. If something fell flat, it might work well for the next team, so be careful about jumping to conclusions too quickly. As you build your facilitation muscles, it will become clearer what skills, processes, and methods need to be adapted in your practice.

Whether you ask for feedback from your team or from your co-facilitator, know that their reflections are invaluable when it comes to developing your skills and your self-awareness as a group facilitator.

CONCLUSION

Maintaining neutrality is a cornerstone principle of skillful facilitation because it is about the organic development of what works best for the group or organization you're working with. It will bring each participant to a deeper level of trust in the group, and that deeper level of trust is where traction and buy-in live with all participants in a team.

Yet this is the principle of facilitation where many feel the most tension. It bubbles up in the space between adding what they *perceive* as value (which is often giving direction and providing content) and stepping back to focus on the group process and group dynamics. Giving the content over to the group is where many new facilitators struggle the most.

So, the work to be done here is to locate the source of your tension within yourself: where does it come from? What is it about? Check the assumptions that you're making about value— and about the group itself! Then, challenge yourself to remain completely neutral from the start.

Own the process. The rest will follow.

CHAPTER 2:

Standing in the Storm

Storms emerge from opposition and high-tension situations within a group process. Storms are places of difference. They are also places of *energy*. You will know you've entered a storm when the emotions are high and the stakes are raised.

While the storm might look, feel, and behave differently with each team, there are certain characteristics within the group dynamic that have a tendency to create them. Messiness, uncertainty, fixed beliefs, hidden assumptions, unwavering opinions or positions, black-and-white thinking, right-or-wrong polarities, power dynamics, hidden agendas...all of these things can create storms.

However, most groups do not naturally want to stay in conflict situations. In fact, they usually have patterns of avoiding them, often at all costs. This facilitation stance is therefore about being able to recognize the storm and understanding how to weather it—because there is greater clarity in a group's thinking on the other side. It is about staying with conflict and difference instead of avoiding it, recognizing that different points of view provide clarity, discernment, deeper understanding, and energy. It is about seeking out and really listening to people's points of view, perspectives, options, solutions, and paths, knowing that collaboration will be less effective without them.

Standing in the storm is about holding space for all to speak and be heard during a meeting even when storms arise.

A STORM ON THE HORIZON

Let me tell you a story about when I was participating in a team chartering session for a volunteer effort. We were not with any one organization. We were just a group of people mobilizing to create a product for the community. Some of us knew one another in other capacities, but mostly we were just getting to know each other. It was a group of very experienced coaches and facilitators. It felt respectful, authentic, and collegial.

And then, quite suddenly, one person made an unexpected move and we could instantly feel the energy in the group rise from the ground. We had found our storm. It was an idea that contained passion and sparked differences within the group. It certainly caught *me* off guard. I knew we were bound to have storms at some point, but I thought they would come later.

Collectively, we stayed with the topic. We chose to stay with whatever discomfort existed for each of us individually, and we worked with the change in group energy. The result was that we came out all the better for it on the other side. Not only were we more collaborative because of the work we did to pull through our storm, we learned to trust our collective ability to have generative, open meetings where difference of opinion could be productively surfaced.

That's the thing about the energy in groups—it's not planned. But it's not inherently negative, either. It's *emergent*. And you have a choice to make in the moment to make space for it. When there's a storm on the horizon, you can go back to "feeling good" as a group, or can stay with the shift in energy and keep going.

Energy and opposition can be indicators of something that's needed or missing in the human system. So, if you stay with it, if you stand in that storm as long as you need to, you just might emerge having found a more collective space for thinking together. When a group makes it through a storm, they gain a collective sense of trust and confidence in one another. They know that they have the capability to get through difficult moments and that what's on the other side can be greatly rewarding.

However, when the stakes go up for a group, they can go up for a facilitator as well. Anxious thoughts creep in:

- *How do I handle this much opposition?*
- *What if we don't achieve what we need to do today?*
- *How will I be viewed?*

When there's a storm on the horizon, it's easy to imagine that the meeting will completely unravel, that you'll be blamed, and that you'll look like an ineffective facilitator.

So, standing in the storm is a place of inner work. It is mastering yourself so that you can stay with a moment of crisis in order for the group to emerge on the other side in a more collective, productive place.

THE LIGHTNING ROD

For facilitators and groups alike, choosing to stand in the storm is fundamentally about how you view difference or conflict. For many of us, we naturally feel inclined to avoid, minimize, or shut down difference and opposing voices. In fact, we tend to shut down anything that raises a threat response for one simple reason: because it feels uncomfortable.

So, the first step of this facilitation stance is learning to recognize when the electricity is starting to crackle. Then it's time to practice being comfortable with feeling uncomfortable.

Common storms are those where people in the group hold different viewpoints or opinions about the topic on the table. Imagine this common scenario: there is a development team trying to prioritize the work for their next release. In the meeting, two people are holding on tightly to their individual—and conflicting—beliefs about why Feature A and Feature B should or should not be included.

Now, imagine you are facilitating this conversation. You might notice that the air in the room feels stagnant, that there are only two or three people speaking, and that the majority of people have become silent. You might "feel" the tension. You might even see people actively disengaging—checking their phones, pushing their chairs back, looking at the floor rather than at others. There may even be one person who chimes in and tries to relieve the tension by saying the dispute is not that important: "Let's just include both!" or, "I think we can just move on..."

Within this storm, there are several choices you might make that feel "easy" as the facilitator. They might even feel effective. For example:

- *You can change the topic of the conversation.*
- *You can shut the conversation down.*
- *You can ask the group how important it is to resolve the issue right now. If it can wait, you can ask the group for permission to put the issue in a "parking lot" and save it for a later conversation.*
- *You can take a vote to determine how the majority of people in the room want to proceed.*

But be careful! There is a major downside to all of these options: you are bypassing the opportunity for a deeper conversation.

There is the topic that the group is talking about in the moment, but there is also the *real* issue on the table. The *real* issue is the one that's underlying the conversation. Is it really just about the relative importance of Features A and B? Or, have Features A and B become the replacement topic for something deeper? They may be the lightning rod for something that one or more people in the group do not feel safe talking about. If you bypass the deeper conversation, you will more than likely find yourself back here again, stuck in the same conflict.

Teams form habits around their conversational patterns. If a team's habit is to not talk about the real issue, that is what they will most likely continue to do.

FINDING YOUR FEET

When you encounter a storm like the one described above, your first action must be to resist your own desire to flee. If *you* don't stay in the conversation, why would the group you're facilitating?

This is where the inner work comes into play. How do you naturally respond to uncomfortable situations? With self-awareness in the moment, what might you do instead? Down below, Lesson 1 of this chapter will help you develop ways to stay in the moment regardless of your first impulse.

Your second action should be to get curious.

Listen intently to what's being said and start to make group inquiries. During the conversation, you might ask questions like:

- *What do others think about Features A and B?*
- *Who sees the issue the same way?*
- *Who sees it differently?*
- *What's true about what you're hearing said?*
- *What's at risk if we don't prioritize these two features for the new release?*
- *What else might these features impact?*

If questions like these don't seem to be getting at the real issue, you might just point that out!

Ideally, you will stay with this conversation long enough to get a sense of what the real issue is. And once you get a handle on what's really going on, you can make a more informed decision about what you want your next action as facilitator to be:

- *If it's just about deepening the group understanding about Features A and B, then stay with the conversation.*
- *If it seems to be something else, you might name what you're experiencing: "I'm noticing we're not moving forward in this conversation. I wonder if this circular conversation is about something else entirely. What's getting in the way?"*
- *If it's something that requires more safety, then use a process that creates anonymity and allows people to say what they are thinking without having to voice it. For example, ask everyone to write their greatest concern on an index card and pass it to the facilitator. The facilitator can then take the themes they're reading in the index cards and introduce them back into the group conversation.*

Sometimes, it turns out that a storm is actually a reaction to the process of participating in the facilitated meeting itself. You might find yourself kicking off a meeting or workshop with the sense that all is going well, when suddenly someone raises the concern that this is just a waste of time and they want to get back to their "real work." They don't need any of this "touchy-feely" collaboration stuff. They feel sure that everything will work much faster if the team just gets going on whatever it is that needs to be done.

As a facilitator, this scenario can feel like an attack on you. It can feel particularly uncomfortable when the storm is about your very presence in the room and the value of the work you have come there to do.

So, what do you do in this situation?

You could shut down the person and thank them for their feedback. But this approach will likely encourage the person to get more vocal as the meeting goes on.

Try these steps instead:

- *Seperate yourself from the process of the meeting. The facilitator and the process for the meeting are not one and the same.*
- *Take a step back and ask if there are any others who have concerns or similar opinions. Let each person who wants to speak say just a bit about what's happening for them or what they are concerned about.*
- *When it feels like enough has been said and the energy is lowering, then slow down your own cadence and ask, "Can I ask you a question?" Wait for someone to respond before you continue. "What would you need to believe was going to happen today in order to be willing to be here in this process?" Again, let people respond. Capture what's said on a flipchart.*
- *Step back and look at the desired outcomes. Do they align with the overall purpose? If so, then ask, "If we agree to these outcomes, are you willing to give this process a try?"*

♦ *For those that don't align with the overall purpose of the meeting, ask if you can place their concerns in a parking lot and set up another meeting to address them.*

Storms are those places when working with a group feels uncomfortable. For you or for them. For one person or for the whole group. But standing in it together is a profound way to transform discomfort into something more productive and thoughtful.

STARTING THE PRACTICE

Not so long ago, a newly-minted facilitator was leading a large workshop of thirty-five participants from different groups across a very large organization. There were multiple stakeholder groups represented in the room, each with their own agenda regarding the decision to be made.

The group was stuck in debate. Heat was high, emotions were fraught, and there was very little alignment. And then, the sponsor and ultimate decision maker in the room slammed his hand on the table. He said, "I'm not comfortable with where this is going, and we're going to stop this conversation here and now." With that, he shoved his chair back and left the room.

In hindsight, the facilitator could clearly see that there was an underlying issue that was larger than the topic being discussed. But in the moment, the facilitator was frozen and sweating. Their heart was pounding and they were completely uncertain of what to do. The room had been full of debate and conflict seconds ago, and now it was just stone-cold silence. Did he do something wrong? Should he make a move? Should he ask the group what to do? Should he keep going and pretend that guy didn't just have a temper tantrum in front of all of these people? Should they take a break?

All the typical feelings of insecurity came flooding forward for this facilitator. He said to himself, "See, I should never have agreed to work with this group. I'm clearly not qualified enough." He began to search the room for someone, anyone, who could be an ally and help save him from the complete breakdown he was experiencing in this situation.

Then, he took a deep breath and said, "Let's stop here for a moment and take a break."

He went out of the room to speak to the sponsor, where he learned that the sponsor wanted him, as the facilitator, to change the topic. The sponsor remained in disagreement with the direction the conversation had taken and stood firm in his desire to simply shut it down.

When the facilitator reconvened the meeting, he honored the sponsor's request by moving the group on to a different topic altogether.

This story is such a great example of a storm. There was high heat, there were high stakes, and there was a lot of energy. In a situation like this, there are no right or wrong ways to navigate the meeting, but there are intentional choices to make that lead to more or less productive outcomes.

Lesson 1: Cultivate self-awareness and management to stay in the situation

In the scenario above, the sponsor requested that the facilitator move on from the high-heat topic altogether. Because the facilitator complied, this group missed the opportunity to carry their conversations to the next level—a place of more informed understanding around differing perspectives. Furthermore, the group likely learned a lesson about norms in this setting. They likely learned that differences of opinion and perspective would not be welcomed in the space, and that compliance and agreement would get rewarded.

People likely learned that speaking their true thoughts would be a waste of time.

What if...

What if this newly minted facilitator had taken a different path. What if he had said to the sponsor:

> "I'm hearing that the conversation has wandered into a space you're not comfortable with. That's totally fine. You get to make that call. However, I need for you to find the words for how you want to share that with the group so that they will understand what's happening and why we are going to move on from this conversation. If I just reconvene the meeting and change the subject, that's going to leave residue on this group. They won't know what's happened and might spend the rest of the meeting thinking they have done something wrong. I need you to come back in and be clear about the following things:
>
> ⬧ *What are you hearing? What's happening for you right now?*
> ⬧ *What's the boundary that's being crossed and why?*
> ⬧ *What's the next step for this topic?*"

What if the facilitator had then helped the sponsor determine the clearest way to communicate with his team? It might sound something like this:

> "I [the sponsor] am hearing lots of passion and energy around this topic and it's clearly something that you're

70

all very vested in. I'm not at liberty to make a decision about this and that instruction has been given to me by my leadership. I don't want us to continue this conversation because I'm worried that it might give the impression that this group will get to have input on this. I would like to move us away from this conversation right now so we don't use our valuable time together talking about something we can't influence. I will take your concerns back to my leadership, and I would be willing to share any updates with this group once I have something."

In this alternate scenario, what the facilitator is asking for is more **context**. They are asking for the individual context (the sponsor's personal perspective) so that the group can understand why the sponsor reacted the way they did *and* why the topic is off limits.

If the first step is establishing context, the next step is **clarifying what happens moving forward**. What will happen to this topic? Who will make the decision, by when, and how will the group know?

The important thing to recognize when learning to stand in the storm is that staying with situations and group dynamics can feel difficult. So start practicing in small ways to help you prepare you for the big moment.

If you run into a situation with a group where your immediate reaction is to change the topic or take a break, practice being curious instead! Make a statement of fact, without judgement, about what's happening in the room. And then just ask a simple question about it. For example: "It seems like there is a lot of heat around this topic. What's creating the energy?"

And remember: we can't go back in time. So, it's important to establish some sort of self-reflection (like journaling) to help you develop your capacity. Carve out time after a meeting to reflect on what happened during a storm:

- *What did you do?*
- *What were you aiming to achieve in that moment?*
- *What was the impact of your action?*
- *What are some other ways you might have acted?*

Lesson 2: Learn to press "pause"

Sometimes what's needed in the midst of a storm is your own personal "pause" button.

You'll know when you need it. Because when you feel like slowing down and taking a breath is the very *last* thing you can do, it's exactly what you *need* to do. The trick is learning to recognize these moments and to be prepared to take your pause even when it feels like the hardest thing:

- *Plant your feet firmly on the ground and stand with the principles of this facilitation stance.*
- *Take a deep breath.*
- *Remember that whatever is happening is not really about you. It's about them.*
- *Slow down the pace for yourself.*

Once you've taken your own pause, you can come back to the group with more grounding to help them through their process. You can help them slow down, too, so they can explore what's happening in their group.

You might try this:

- *In a really slow and deliberate manner, say, "Can I ask you a question?"*

     ❖ *When you receive a vocalized response, simply ask: "What's happening right now?"*

As the group responds, gather the data about what's happening for them. This will help you decide what's needed next. Remember: you don't have to figure out the next four things. You just need to figure out the one thing that will move the group forward in this moment.

Lesson 3: Deepen your understanding of group dynamics (learn a model for conflict)

Models and frameworks for understanding group dynamics help us make sense of what we're experiencing in the room. They also help us get out of our own heads. After all, it's not about us!

In Chapter 1, I offered specific recommendations for models and frameworks you can familiarize yourself with in order to anchor your understanding of group dynamics. Now, as you're developing your ability to stand in a storm, let's dig into the model that will specifically help you hold this stance.

Structural Dynamics is a theory of face-to-face communication developed by David Kantor.[9] It provides a way of naming, at four different levels, the structure of communication as it's taking place in the moment. It's a behavioral model that is morally neutral, meaning that there is no "bad" or "good." There is no judgment about how you are communicating now and how you need to be communicating in the future. It's just a way of saying "here's what's happening in this moment...is it working for you?"

The first level of Structural Dynamics encompasses the action modes. The action modes provide a way of coding conversation to reveal patterns that might be helping—or hindering—a

---

9   See Kantor, *Reading the Room.*

group trying to make progress. In order for conversation to be skillful and effective, groups need all four of the following actions to be voiced in conversation:

- **Move:** *this action sets the direction in a conversation.*
- **Follow:** *this action supports the Move and continues the line of thinking.*
- **Oppose:** *this action offers a correction or a different perspective.*
- **Bystand:** *this action brings a morally neutral perspective on what's happening in the conversation, or it bridges competing ideas.*

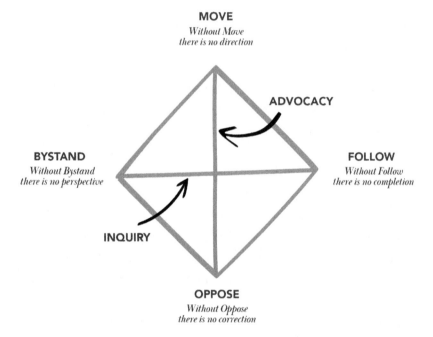

A common pattern in teams is that one or more of these actions will either be missing from the conversation or not used when it's needed. When it comes to conflict—those moments where we find ourselves standing in the storm—we're often experiencing the effect of an Oppose action being voiced in the room. For new facilitators just starting out, it can be tempting to limit or manage the voice of opposition. But, instead of limiting this voice or looking for a way to make it go away, it's important to reframe your relationship to the Oppose action so that you can see it for what it is—a voice for something that's missing or needed in the conversation.

Those who voice an Oppose do so with lots of courage. They often find themselves labeled "the naysayer," "the devil's advocate," or "the difficult one." But these judgments are not helpful, and they put a substantial burden on those individuals. In fact, when an Oppose action is ignored or dismissed, it can grow bigger and take on other behaviors that get in the way of group work. Things like disengagement, silence, showing up late or not at all—these are all signs that the voice of opposition is not being heard within the group. And the issues can get bigger, with individuals becoming argumentative or turning to personal attacks. So, when someone is brave enough to voice an Oppose, it's your job to recognize the action for what it is and welcome it into the conversation.

Looking at conflict through Structural Dynamics helps make sense of and build meaning around its importance and impact in a group setting.

Lesson 4: Create a container for psychological safety

When it comes to the stance of standing in the storm, much of the initial work is self work on your part. But you can also help groups prepare to stand in the storm by introducing them to the idea of a container.

Building a container provides the group with a safe space that has clear boundaries and agreements regarding what they can expect and count on from each other and from the facilitator. A container fosters trust, connection, and inclusiveness. It creates a space of listening, respecting, and suspending judgment. It is a space to relinquish the idea that one person has the answer, and it establishes the belief that it is worth questing for an answer together.

The first step in creating a container is getting to know each other with questions that are focused on hearing from each person:

+ *Who are you as a person?*
+ *What do you value?*
+ *What's important to you?*
+ *What are your individual strengths?*
+ *What brought you to where you are today?*

The next step of building the container is asking questions that are oriented around the collective. These are "we" questions that help build a shared vision for why this group has come together.

+ *What's our highest hope for the experience of working together?*
+ *What's our greatest fear of working together?*
+ *What do we want to achieve together?*
+ *How will we make decisions together?*
+ *What are everyone's roles?*
+ *What assumptions are we making?*
+ *What expectations do we have?*

The primary purpose of a container is to make assumptions and expectations explicit. When we make the implicit more explicit, we build trust in the group and empower group members to take more risks in working with one another. By building a container, groups formulate shared expectations and agreements that they can rely on to guide their group process and help when they inevitably find places of difference.

Here are more questions you can ask:

- *What can we expect from each other?*
- *What do we need in order to realize our highest hopes?*
- *What will we do when we disagree about something?*
- *How will we handle hierarchy?*
- *For a group member who reports to someone else in this room, is it okay for them to disagree with that person while here in this space?*
- *What will we do with technology?*
- *What does it look like to be respectful?*
- *How will we know if we're having fun?*

Once a container is in place, the group is fundamentally more prepared to weather storms within their process. Will they avoid them? No. But they will have a shared vocabulary—a set of agreed upon norms—to help guide them through high-heat moments to a place of deeper understanding on the other side.

CONCLUSION

Simply put, without difference there is no insight, clarity, energy, passion, or conviction. Storms give us these things—which means we have to stay with the storm no matter how uncomfortable it feels. If we move away from conflict or shut it down, the group does not reap the benefit of deeper understanding that they foster and achieve when they move through it. Moreover, storms build trust. When managed well, a storm can strengthen relationships and build collective confidence in the team's ability to get through difficult conversations.

On the other side of the storm lies collective intelligence. So, our job as facilitators is to prepare to effectively stand in the storm. Because it's not *if* the storm happens, it's *when*—and it's how you choose to respond to it in the moment.

CHAPTER 3:

Honoring the Wisdom of the Group

When groups convene, they have the power to create something together that would not be possible from the thinking of just one or two people. Groups can see problems in new ways and craft solutions that weren't apparent before. But the creation of new thinking relies on a group's ability to access their collective intelligence.

Honoring the wisdom of the group, at its core, is about trust. It's about trusting that the group has its own wisdom so that you can help develop an environment where each member of the team can grow, stretch, and achieve as a respected and valued collaborator.

Everyone on the team has both wisdom to gain and wisdom to share.

In theory, honoring the wisdom of the group is really easy. Often, both leaders and group members agree: of course the group has wisdom! Some will have read books like *The Wisdom of Teams* by Jon Katzenbach and Douglas Smith. Others will have first-hand experience of making decisions collectively in a collaborative manner, and they will remember feeling involved—like they owned a piece of the direction and outcome. Still others will just have an intuitive sense that they trust in groups and teams.

But then real life happens. Decisions need to be made. Directions need to be set.

Think about, for example, when a software team needs to make a decision about which architecture to use. Let's say the most senior architect has some ideas, but, collectively, the team disagrees. Some teams might voice their disagreement. Some teams will remain silent and politely defer to the more senior voice in their team. In some cases, the team leader might just take the decision away from the group and make the decision on their own. It's easy to imagine any of these situations, isn't it?

It's often easier to honor the wisdom of the group in principle than it is in the moment. This is what pressure does. In the moment, group members might express a different internal narrative altogether, one that might suggest, for example, that there is nothing useful to be gleaned from groups. That group thinking is a waste of time. For some people, group meetings might trigger a dreadful memory of a group project in high school where they were stuck doing all the work. Their teammates benefited from the grade, but didn't contribute equally to the product. In high-pressure moments, leaders, in particular, might be challenged by the concept of honoring the group's wisdom. They would rather just make the decision on their own and tell the group what to do.

However, just because something takes longer than you might have anticipated does not make it invaluable or not useful. Sometimes, the work we must do as facilitators is to help a team increase its patience.

Really good ideas are often just on the other side of breakdown, frustration, and confusion.

LEADERSHIP AND FACILITATION: WHY BREAKDOWN HAPPENS

Imagine you're a newly hired leader in a large and successful technology firm in Silicon Valley. Your job is to help the organization transform. You've been on the job for about six months. You understand the culture and the details of what's happening in the teams. You clearly see some things that are getting in the way of what the teams and the organization really want, and you've been socializing some new ideas with your team and hoping to get their buy-in as you meet with them individually.

One afternoon, you set up a time to meet with your senior team. You've decided you are going to step into the role of facilitator because there are some conversations you would like this group to have. So, you book the room, plan the agenda, create the purpose statement, and kickoff the meeting. You have been practicing your facilitation stance, so you are committed to maintaining your neutrality and facilitating an open conversation about the coming changes.

And then...you get hooked on the topic. You care greatly about the outcome of this meeting, and you suddenly realize that the data you have collected and the behavior you have observed over the past six months gives you greater insight into the topic than you're hearing from the team. You are sure you are right! You know you have the answers! So, you drop your neutral stance and begin to engage in a debate with the team.

As the team begins to question and challenge what you're sharing, you dig in. You offer up all the data you have and advocate for the course of action you are suggesting. But the team is not having it. While you get louder and more certain, they also get louder and more certain. The meeting has gone off the rails.

In this moment, the group has lost their content-neutral facilitator, their process guide, AND the person who could help them tap into their collective intelligence.

Now, let's imagine the same scenario from the opposite perspective.

Imagine you've been called into a group meeting by the new guy who has only been with your organization for about six months. You like all the interactions you've had with him. He seems genuine, like he's really listening. You notice that he's been sharing some new ideas with everyone, and you're looking forward to engaging in a conversation about what's happening and where all of you as a group might find some new solutions to current challenges.

So when you arrive for the meeting, you're pretty jazzed. You're thinking, "Great! We're finally going to come together and sort things out!" You see an agenda ("Nice! I love that we have a plan!"). You see a very clear purpose hanging on the wall ("Even better! This will help us stay focused!"). You grab a seat, excited to get started.

But after the meeting begins, you start to notice that you're not feeling as energized as you were when you walked in. Your "spidey senses" are starting to tingle a bit. There's just something about this meeting that doesn't feel right. The new guy who's supposed to be facilitating the meeting is sharing a lot of data about what he's seen, but he's not asking many questions. And while you agree with some of what he's saying, some of it...not so much.

You start to wonder if it's just you. Maybe you missed something. But then another team member speaks up, offering an objection to some of the statements being made. The facilitator now becomes actively engaged in a debate with your team member. So, you jump in and offer *your* perspective, backing up your team member's comment. But the facilitator ignores the comments and continues to talk. He begins asserting new ideas about what he thinks should be done, rather than offering up observations for the conversation.

In this moment, you find yourself a bit angry. You're feeling dismissed and misunderstood. Why bother having a conversation if you're just going to be told what's right? It feels like a waste of your time.

What's happened here?

This imagination exercise walks you through a very common kind of breakdown. It occurs when a facilitator—whether they are an outside facilitator, agile coach, team leader, or group member who has taken on one of these roles—fails to honor the wisdom of the group.

Facilitation is about believing and trusting that the group has everything they need—including the collective intelligence and ability to solve for anything. A common trap for facilitators (or team members who step into that role) is that they begin to question or doubt their belief in the group's ability. You will know this is happening if you begin to notice thoughts like:

- *"Well, they don't have all the data I have"*
- *"I just need to help them see it my way"*
- *"This is all wrong, they don't get it"*
- *"This group is too young, they don't have the experience or the data to make this decision"*
- *"We don't have time for this, I clearly just need to make a decision so we can move forward"*

Several things are happening simultaneously. You are starting to see your *own* agenda emerge, you are stepping out of neutrality, and you are starting to believe that the group needs you to "do it for them."

When you're not honoring the wisdom of the group, it's the equivalent of walking up to someone and taking their work away from them because it's not being done the way you would do it. It's disempowering, it's micromanaging, and it's not sustainable. And the results are predictable. People walk out of the meeting feeling everything that makes them hate meetings:

- *They're not being heard*
- *They're not being understood*
- *They're wasting their time*

CREATING A SPACE FOR EVERYONE IN THE GROUP

Here's a concern I often hear when it comes to honoring the wisdom of the group: *"My team really does not have wisdom. They are new to this work and lack the insight and experience needed to make better decisions."*

The assumption behind this thinking is that the group needs a facilitator or leader to tell them what they don't know. But the cornerstone principle of honoring the wisdom of the group is that they *don't* need to be told. It's that the group has everything it already needs, and the facilitator needs to trust the group to name for themselves what they need to reach a decision or solution.

The next concern I often hear is, *"But what if they don't name what they need? What if they just remain silent?"*

This is a separate issue. If a team remains silent, it is not about wisdom or lack of wisdom, but about not having an environment and culture that supports the group in voicing their needs. It's a leadership and cultural issue, not a wisdom issue. The wisdom is there, but it's buried under the norms and patterns telling group members that it's not okay to contribute their voices.

When the collective wisdom of the group is not voiced, there is work to do.

The first step is to get curious: what patterns and norms are contributing to this team not being able to ask for what they need? Why don't they feel comfortable voicing their opinions?

Depending on the answer, your work as a facilitator may alter course. This is where you will need to hold the group's agenda (see Chapter 4) and help them untangle the group dynamic.

When the group is ready to voice their needs with more comfort, the next step is to ask the group what's missing for them. Ask them what they need to come to a decision or to move forward with their conversation. Maybe they need training. Maybe they are lacking data. In some cases, you may even discover that what's at stake does not warrant a collaborative decision! There's no good way to move the conversation forward until a group can express their collective wisdom.

One of our most important jobs as facilitators is to help create a space where all voices can be heard. It is to create a space premised on the belief that taking the time to create and tap into collective intelligence is worth it—and that the results will be greater than any individual idea. It is to cultivate a belief that the trust created through the conversation will spill over into other work the team does. It is to honor the belief that a diversity of options and experiences—of different ways of looking at the same problem—will reveal a generative outcome that no one person could have created on their own.

To create this space, we must deepen our understanding of how our internal assumptions and beliefs inform our behaviors in the room. We must learn to *recognize* when we are honoring the wisdom of the group, as well as when we aren't.

Honoring vs. not honoring group wisdom—what it looks and feels like for facilitators

HONORING THE WISDOM OF THE GROUP

Internal assumptions and beliefs

- I trust in the collective intelligence, capacity, and experience of the group
- I recognize that people are more committed to what they have helped create
- I believe that the whole is greater than the sum of its parts
- I believe that diversity and difference enhance the outcome
- I recognize how important it is to include and engage everyone in the room
- Connecting a group builds trust, which leads to an environment more conducive to participation by all
- I believe that the group already has everything it needs; my job is to help them access their knowledge and be able to ask for what they need when they need it
- If we close the process down too soon, we might miss something
- People will feel shut off and not included if we stop here

Practices in the room

- I create containers that foster trust, connection, and inclusiveness
- I help the group see the value of hearing different perspectives and why opposition is critical to group conversation
- I design group processes that engage the whole group
- I am watching for signs of psychological safety or lack of safety and factor that into my designs
- I help the group make space for all voices
- I ask for the opposing voice and help the group do the same
- I find the thread that leads to consensus, then help the group to pull it through

	NOT HONORING THE WISDOM OF THE GROUP
Internal assumptions and beliefs	• This group has no wisdom - they are too young, inexperienced, lack data, lack knowledge,
	• If left to their own devices, this group would make all the wrong decisions or no decision at all
	• I already know the best solution, if they would just listen to me
Practices in the room	• I allow the group to get stuck in Exporation, with no time given to Evaluating and Deciding
	• I cut off conversations when I, or someone in the group, becomes uncomfortable with the topic
	• I advocate for the answer I think is best rather than allowing the group to come to their best decision
	• I passively allow the group to make a bad decision for the sake of honoring their "so-called" wisdom

Remember: when you honor the wisdom of the group, you are creating the space for them to do their best, most collaborative work. This is the space of true innovation and progress.

WORDS OF CAUTION

Collaborative decision making is very powerful. It's powerful for cultivating involvement and engagement, when you want people to take action from a place of inspiration and alignment, and when there is great complexity and no easy answer. In short, collaborative decision-making is powerful when you need group buy-in and when two heads are better than one.

But there are some moments when it may not be appropriate. Not every decision must be made in a collaborative, collective manner or with the aid of a facilitator. So, it is important to recognize when, where, and why a different model of decision-making is appropriate. After all, part of honoring the wisdom of the group is understanding how to honor their time in a group process.

The over-collaboration trap

Sometimes, a group learning to be more collaborative can swing the pendulum all the way over to the other side and start believing that *everything* needs to be decided by consensus (meaning that everyone can live with and support the decision). But this is not always appropriate. For example, I was once working with a leadership team where the leader's preference was for an open system in which the input of all voices would be heard. There were very few places where he was willing to take a stand for something. He wanted to take everything to the team.

In some ways, the team appreciated this, they wanted to be consulted on things that would impact them, and they trusted this leader to always bring those topics to them. But what was also happening for this team was that they were stuck. They were spinning. There were always lots of ideas and opinions on the table about various topics, yet they were unable to move *forward* on much of anything.

This leader and his team were stuck in the trap of *servant leadership*. They *wanted* to be of service to each other, always, but they were overdoing it and couldn't move forward.

Overdoing the idea of servant leadership is only one way to fall into the trap of over-collaboration. In a very different scenario, I worked with a team that was convinced that their leader was only interested in bringing them together for "collaboration theater." This is a great phrase coined by Ben Tinker to describe the act of a leader *pretending* they want a collaborative decision when, in truth, they already had an answer. Or, in the case of the team I was working with, it can look like the leader having data that the rest of the team did not—and therefore being the only person actually equipped to reach a sound decision.

Sometimes, it would just be better for everyone if the leader asserted the idea that they want to act on and then let the team voice any concerns. In fact, there are times when the group might actually feel like their leader would be better able to make a decision based on their experience and perspective. So, leading the team through a long process that feels like staging a show? No one will buy into the outcome.

The "something's missing" trap

If it feels like a group is spinning their wheels and that they may not share your belief in their collective wisdom, then it's time for you to inquire about what (or who) is missing. Because honoring the wisdom of the group includes honoring their ability to ask for what they need or state what they think is absent.

One of the biggest challenges groups face is not having the right people or all the necessary information accounted for in the room. If you're planning for a conversation about architecture but you don't have the architect in the room, for example, then someone is missing. And the "something's missing" trap can lead to wasted time and frustration for the team.

Planning for full engagement and participation starts before the meeting. Once the purpose is defined, do some work to determine who or what should—and who or what shouldn't—be there. Questions that will help you make this assessment include:

- *What information or context is needed for the conversation to unfold productively?*
- *Who will be impacted by the outcome of the meeting?*
- *Who will need to be both aware of and bought-in to the final decisions?*

The takeaway here is that, when it comes to honoring the wisdom of the group, understanding the dynamic of who—or what—needs to be present is part of your work.

Wisdom exists, we just collectively create a lot of shenanigans that block it from coming forward. Trust that the group has what they need or that you can turn the conversation back to them to state what's missing.

It is not your job to solve things for the group. It *is* your job to help them create the conditions that will help them to solve it for themselves.

STARTING THE PRACTICE

Honoring the wisdom of the group means placing your full attention on what the group needs rather than focusing on your own needs. It starts with being deliberate about why you are meeting and how you can help invite full participation by creating and sustaining a space that will support it.

The practices of honoring the wisdom in the group build directly on the practices begun in the last chapter. For example, remember that container you learned to create in Chapter 2? It's not just important for helping a team stand in the storm, it's also critical for creating the environment where people feel comfortable contributing to the conversation. A container is a cornerstone practice for helping a group tap into its collective intelligence by creating space for every voice.

So, as you move forward in this chapter, try combining the practices here with what you have already learned.

What you may notice in the following section is that the first three lessons are a bit more prescriptive. They offer specific guidance about how to plan and design a collaborative meeting and set the group up for success. This specificity is designed to help new facilitators escape the trap of low expectations that can exist around the role of facilitation. Many organizations just see facilitation as a very basic set of skills: if you invite people to the meeting, reserve the room, and send out an agenda ahead of time—then, you've done it. You're facilitating! More often than not, people walk into a meeting and just "wing it." They make it up as they go without much thought regarding the meeting's purpose, objectives, or their own power as meeting facilitator to either propel or block effective collaboration. As facilitators, we can do better.

These first three practices are here to help you define the purpose of the meeting and be very intentional about why you would meet in the first place.

Lesson 1: Help the sponsor get clear on the level of collaboration needed

One way we honor wisdom in groups is by not wasting their time. Being intentional and deliberate about when collaborative decision-making is an appropriate process to meet the needs of the moment—and when someone just needs to make a decision and move forward.

Many leaders buy into the idea that "people will support what they help to create," so much so that they make every decision a collaborative process. Which ends up being collaboration over-done. It leads to collaboration theater, where the decision has mostly been made but we're just going to go through the motions of collaboration.

I love open, collaborative processes. I often say it's in my DNA to seek input from others. Part of *my* work to do as a leader has been to clarify when I am really open to others having input and when my thinking is pretty clear and I'm not as open to input. Not every decision needs an open conversation. There will be times when one person needs to make a decision and you'll just inform the rest of the group and seek their input on risks and actions as needed.

As a facilitator, one of the most important conversations you can have is with the sponsor in the planning phase of the meeting. Revisit the Planning and Design for Facilitation practices introduced in Chapter 1, Lesson 1: Know before you go. The key element here is the sponsor interview. The meeting's sponsor is the person that stands to gain the most from the outcome. This will be the person(s) who can determine the degree of collaboration and the type of decision the group will be making.

WHAT TYPE OF MEETING IS IT?

Ad Hoc	Status	Working	Planning	Strategic / Innovative
Informal Brief Conversation	*Structured Informational*	*Understanding the issue*	*Gathering information*	*Envisioning the future*
A Few People	*One-way*	*Problem solving*	*Need for consensus*	*Creating new*
		Making decisions	*Multiple stakeholders*	*Multiple stakeholders*

Low ⟶ High

Degrees of Collaboration/Facilitation

Factors to determine the degree of collaboration

Honoring the wisdom of the group is a cornerstone of collaborative decision-making, but not every topic, problem, or decision needs to be collaborative. Higher complexity in decisions means a greater degree of collaboration will be important. When you are interviewing the sponsor and evaluating the complexity of a decision to be made, think about the scope:

    ♦ **Urgency**
        How quickly does the decision need to be made?

- **Risk**

  What's at risk? Risks are uncertain events that might take place. Higher risk means there is a higher probability that certain events may happen, which means there is more benefit to be had from collaborative thinking and seeking multiple stakeholders' perspectives.

- **Impact**

  What's the scope of the decision's impact? Does the decision impact one person, a whole team, a department, the entire organization? Greater impact means higher complexity and makes having diverse voices and thinking more important.

- **Durability**

  How long does the decision need to last? Does it need to last a day? A week? A month? The longer it needs to last, the more important collaboration becomes during the decision-making process.

- **Buy-in**

  How important is it that others buy in into the decision that's being made? How much ownership do they need to feel in the decision? The greater the need for buy-in, the greater the need for a collaborative decision-making process.

People will support what they help to create. In the age of knowledge work, having input into a process, understanding how a decision came to be, and knowing the thinking behind it will go a long way toward people actively playing their part in making it happen.

Use the above criteria to help you and the sponsor determine whether collaborative decision-making is appropriate, and, if it is, continue into your planning and design process for the facilitation.

Lesson 2: Decide how to decide

Not every decision lends itself to consensus, and that's okay. It often depends on the type and complexity of the decision being made. The key is to be clear and upfront with the group about what the decision-making process will be.

If someone else is ultimately going to make the final decision and the group is simply going to make a recommendation, be clear about it from the beginning. There is nothing more frustrating to a group than to become highly invested and bought into a decision only to learn at the end of the meeting (or a week later) that a leader over-rode their decision and changed it. That's a fast path to lack of trust in the process and a distaste for collaborative processes.

So, help the sponsor and other stakeholders agree to both the decision-making process and the boundaries of the decision prior to the meeting.

Types of Decisions:

* **Leader Decides**
  The leader hears the dialogue and input from the group and then makes the decision.

* **Leader Holds Veto Power**
  The group makes a decision but the leader holds the final decision and can veto or override the group's proposal.

⬥ **Consensus Building**

"I can live with and support it." The group comes to consensus on the decision.

⬥ **Majority Rule**

The group makes a decision based on the majority of the group agreeing to the proposal.

A word of caution: Teams often default to "majority rules," likely because reaching consensus can take more time and some teams or leaders become frustrated with the process. From a facilitation perspective, brainstorming ideas is the easy part. Hearing all voices, making space for opposition, evaluating, narrowing, and deciding are the trickier parts of group work.

If you use "majority rules" (e.g., dot voting and selecting the item with the most votes) as your primary way of making decisions, you might be missing opportunities to uncover more insight and wisdom, which could improve the shared vision, increase understanding, and change the nature of the conversation and outcomes more positively over time. While appropriate for some decisions, "majority rules" can easily be overused.

Lesson 3: Design group processes that invite all voices

Your objective here is to design a way for all voices to be heard in the room. This is a key element of honoring the group's wisdom, and it happens in two ways. The first is to have a plan for how you will *get* all the voices in the room—how you will get everyone involved. The second is more figurative—making sure that everyone *has* a say, even if they are not speaking aloud in the moment.

Factors to consider in your design include:

- *What's the purpose of the meeting?*
- *What's the desired outcome?*
- *How many people are participating?*
- *Will others be observing? If so, what might the impact of that be on those who are participating?*
- *How will you be meeting (e.g., in person or online)?*
- *How long do you have?*

Once you have these factors determined, it's time to create your facilitation design.

Create the arc

- **Identify the outcome:**
  When designing an arc for your facilitation, you're looking at creating the meeting's journey—the path that will help the participants get to where they need to go.

  To design your arc, start with the end in mind: what's the desired outcome for this meeting? Be clear about whether this meeting is being held to explore, evaluate, and/or make a decision. Starting with the desired outcome is a way to "chunk up" the planning process into concrete pieces that are easier to work with while keeping the overall arc of your meeting firmly in mind.

◆ **Create an agenda in question format:**

Once you've identified the desired outcome of the meeting, the next step is to design questions that the group will need to answer in order to get there. These questions form the arc itself— getting the group from Point A to Point Z as productively as possible.

Have you ever received a meeting agenda that looked like this?
  ◦ Discuss the options for our strategy
  ◦ Check in on the status of actions
  ◦ Remaining budget items

◆ **Decide what's next**

As a participant in this meeting, I'd have no clue what is expected of me, how I could prepare, or what thinking would be helpful prior to the meeting.

Now, look at this agenda:

1. *What impact might we have next year if cost was not a factor?*
2. *How might we allocate our budget for the highest impact ideas?*
3. *How does our current work correlate to the new ideas?*
4. *How committed are we to the highest impact ideas?*
5. What's the next most important action to take?

As a participant in this meeting, I'd be excited by the first question and could begin to consider and think freely about what I would like to propose. I'd feel intrigued by the other questions, too, because I would see the flow of how our thinking together might evolve over the course of the meeting. I'd appreciate knowing in advance what questions would be posed to me so that I could prepare accordingly.

Creating agendas in question format draws people into collaboration, engages their brain, and helps participants get started on the meeting—all before the meeting even starts.

Level the playing field

Whether you are co-located and meeting in a shared room or you are remote and meeting online, it's important to level the playing field. Think about the power dynamics that are naturally inherent in any group. Power comes from an individual's role, status, seniority, knowledge, etc. When the power is out of balance, it changes how people participate and can inadvertently give more power to some and less to others.

Think about your average conference room with a rectangular table. Those seated at either end of the table have the advantage of being able to see most people clearly, and most people around the table can easily make eye contact with them. By contrast, those seated along the sides of the rectangle will have a hard time seeing people who are seated on their same side of the table. This basic table configuration automatically shifts the power to those seated at either end of the table.

Another common example is in a blended session where some of the group is co-located and others are attending virtually. In this situation, the power will reside in the group that is co-located. Without conscious attention to how to include the voices online, the power dynamic will be out of balance and participants' voices will not all be heard equally.

Leveling the playing field gives attention to understanding what dynamics might be at play in the room and creating a design so that **everyone is on equal footing and can participate with equal voice.** Practical ways to do this include:

In the room:

- *Using round tables*
- *Removing tables in the room and having everyone sit in a circle*
- *Asking people to stand up and move around the room to a space that is not around a table*

Online:

- *If one person is online, everyone is online*
- *One video and microphone per person*
- *Design for "video on and mute off" to promote more natural engagement and group conversation*

Frames

In a facilitation process, the frames are the group processes that participants will be using to move through the arc of the meeting toward the identified outcome. Changing the frame that people are working in helps people remain engaged and focused on the conversation, which in turn helps to maximize the collaboration.

Types of frames you can use in your design include:

- *Individual writing or reflection*
- *Pair conversation*
- *Trio group work/conversation*
- *Quad group work/conversation*
- *Large-group conversation*
- *Whole-group conversation*

♦ *Debriefing and/or sharing back (this can be done silently, by focusing on specific themes, or in a whole-group conversation)*
♦ *Written pre-work*
♦ *Geography and spatialization (e.g., placing items on the floor or in a virtual whiteboard and "voting with your feet")*

As you design your facilitation, keep in mind that it's important to change the frame of the group process frequently. You are designing so no one person is monologuing (when a solo voice speaks while everyone else listens) for a long period of time. Groups will become exhausted when the same frame is used repeatedly. Changing it up also helps to engage all voices without everyone having to speak or share in the same way.

Adapting the design

The next stage of design comes into play once you are in the room and can read what's happening there. This means that you need to practice *not* being married to your design. Your design is not written in stone. You will need to adapt the process to fit new circumstances as they emerge.

Imagine that I've asked the group to talk about a topic in smaller groups before sharing back with the group at large. In the moment, however, I notice that the sharing feels flat, like there is no energy at all. This is where I need to stop and inquire about what's happening. I need to say something like, "I notice the energy feels flat. What's happening for you right now?"

Now, imagine someone responds with, "In our group, we didn't come up with any really good insights." Someone else says that they ran out of time and were not done yet.

Ah-ha! Mystery solved.

Now that you know what's going on (a group felt uninspired, or ran out of time, or maybe wasn't even clear what they were supposed to be doing), you can adapt your process. You can give them more time. You can rotate individuals between the groups so they can hear the conversations happening between other people. What would get the juices flowing again? Be ready to try different things.

In short, when the design needs to adapt, you need to be prepared to adapt it. That's how you engage everyone and hold space for the wisdom of the group to emerge.

> The primary question across the design process is:
> **What is the highest and best use
> of our time together?**

Lesson 4: Invite opposition—and separate yourself from the process

Opposition is needed in a group in order to have an effective dialogue and, therefore, to access the wisdom of the group in full. So, be thankful when someone is willing to voice it! Acknowledge them for their courage—don't try to make it go away.

Inviting opposition builds on the practices introduced in the last chapter, Standing in the Storm. When applying these same skills to the practice of honoring the group's wisdom, you are simply further developing your capacity to *invite* and *encourage* opposition.

There are two fundamental principles of inviting opposition:

  • *If opposition is not coming into the conversation organically, ask for someone who sees the topic differently.*

101

◆ *When opposition does emerge, don't shut it down!*

If we apply Structural Dynamics, teams where the action of Oppose is missing or underused will notice a pattern in which the Move action is overused. This is called Serial Moving. When this pattern emerges, new topics are frequently introduced in the course of conversation before any correction, observation, or alignment is made to the previous Move. Conversations like this will often have lots of ideas and energy, but they will lack forward movement.

Another pattern that emerges when opposition is not voiced is that new ideas (Moves) are followed by silence or by agreement. This pattern, known as Courteous Compliance, does lead to action, but you'll likely find yourself in the conversation again next week because it lacks all the conversational elements needed to fully understand the Move being proposed.

In both of these patterns, Covert Opposition is also happening—simultaneously and beneath the surface. It's not that there is no Oppose, it's just that the Oppose action goes offline. It moves outside the room and happens over chat, text, email, or conversations with friends in the hallway. When the voice of Oppose goes subterranean, that's where it stands to do the most long-term damage within groups.

As the facilitator, it's important for you to find ways to invite the opposition into the conversation. But, as you develop your skills in relation to opposition, it's also important to recognize when and how to separate yourself from the process.

Remember: you are not the process and the process is not you

When opposition emerges, you might hear negative comments about the process: that the meeting is a waste of time, that group members would rather not be there, etc. If you hear these negative thoughts as comments about *you personally*, your choices will become reactive. They will be driven by ego or the need to protect yourself.

Notice when your thoughts turn to yourself, to your fears about how you might be perceived. It might sound like an inner voice saying, "The group will view me as incompetent or unskillful." When you listen to this voice, you risk defending the process and trying to convince others that the current approach is the best model for moving forward. You might even accidentally cut someone off who is offering an unwelcome viewpoint. In some cases, you might simply become apathetic about the outcome and fall back, letting the group take control of the process.

Instead, stand with your attention on the group. Focus just on this group and tune out all other distractions. Listen to the dynamics that are emerging in the group and the meta view of what you're hearing its members talk about. Then, lean on what you now know about group dynamics—and about yourself. You are not the process, and you **can** separate yourself from it in order to surface the source of the issue at hand.

It's also important to know when you're out over your skis. If you don't feel like you can work with the level of opposition alone, call for help. Get a co-facilitator to come into the room with you. This means finding someone inside or outside your organization who is skillful in working with conflict. Not only are they a resource for you in the moment, you can learn to deepen your own skills by observing them in action.

Keeping the focus on the group and *their* process allows opposition—regardless of how it's initially expressed—to lead the way toward deeper wisdom and understanding.

CONCLUSION

Sometimes we can be really good at creating a vision for what we want: teamwork, collaboration, agility. But in the execution, we can be really good at getting in our own way.

One of the most powerful beliefs you can hold as a facilitator is that the team has the wisdom it needs, even when it feels difficult. Even if the road is bumpy and it feels like you took the wrong exit, holding firm in this stance is one of the most empowering things you can do for a team. Over time, it builds their capacity. It helps team members learn that they can get through difficult conversations. It helps them understand that if they abandon their roles of wisdom—even for a moment— no one else is going to step in and take over, so they would be better served to keep at it.

This is how teams get better at being teams. And as a facilitator, this is one of the greatest gifts you can bring the group.

CHAPTER 4:

Holding the Group's Agenda

If you have ever gotten the feeling that a group is resisting the decision they are narrowing in toward or responding with reluctance toward every attempt to move the meeting forward, you are likely encountering the tension between two unspoken but competing agendas in the room. In these moments, you need to decide if you're going to stick to what the group is *supposed* to be doing in the meeting or if you're going to take a pause and edge into the group dynamic that must be addressed for the meeting to continue productively and collaboratively.

The principle of holding the group's agenda is about continually asking, "How can I best serve this group?" It is about wondering, "What does this group really need right now?" It's letting *your* agenda take the backseat so that you can help a group tackle emergent dynamics. It's about uncovering what's *really* going on in the group so that they can move forward as a team.

This chapter introduces three levels of group agendas, addresses when and how to hold the group's agenda, and helps you meet whatever feelings come up (for you and for the group) with curiosity and focus. When you find yourself able to hold this stance as you facilitate a group process, you will be better prepared to help groups get to the bottom of the entrenched dynamics that are holding them back.

THE THREE GROUP AGENDAS

The first step when it comes to holding the group's agenda is to understand that there are three different levels of agendas that a group can have: the presenting agenda, the emergent agenda, and the developmental agenda.

The presenting agenda:

The *presenting* agenda encompasses the meeting's purpose, desired outcomes, and plan. It is why the group has come together, and it includes the facilitation design anticipated to help the group achieve what it hopes to achieve.

When the group is more tactically focused on the outcome of the meeting, they are focused on the presenting agenda. The group will feel "on task."

The emergent agenda:

The *emergent* agenda is what emerges live in the room as conversations happen, new perspectives are voiced, and ideas are generated. New thinking is often behind the emergence of this new level of group agenda.

Emergent agendas can feel like a tangent or beyond the scope of the meeting's purpose, but there are times when the emergent agenda actually needs to be explored so that the group can reach their desired outcome.

The developmental agenda:

The *developmental* agenda is a deeper agenda that focuses on how the group works together. It's about group behavior and dynamics. Facilitators working with agile teams are not just trying to help a group achieve an outcome for a meeting, they are often helping a team develop. When a group is able to attend to how they work together—not just what they are trying to achieve—they become more aware and are able to be more effective. In fact, focusing on the developmental agenda can actually (and ideally) reduce a group's reliance on a facilitator altogether.

While it's not always within the scope of a facilitated meeting to work on the deeper developmental agenda, it's nevertheless very helpful for the group to name the developmental agenda so they can identify a time to explore it further.

It's one thing to know that there are three levels of agendas that may be at play in the room when you begin a facilitation process, but it will be easier to identify them in the moment if you're ready for it. So, let's imagine you're working with a team meeting for a retrospective. The team members participated in a pre-retro survey, and it revealed a collective theme of wanting to identify ways to improve their work process. This theme therefore becomes the team's *presenting* agenda: the purpose and agenda of the meeting will revolve around reflecting on the current work process and identifying adaptations to the ways that work products could be handed off between one team and another.

During the retrospective meeting, however, a brave conversation between two team members surfaces a challenge in the team dynamics. Jim is frustrated about an incident that had taken place a few weeks back when he had asked two other team members, Ian and Philip, to take the lead on a task and figure out how to make it work.

"I would like to know what's happening with our workflow," says Jim. "I asked Ian and Philip to work on this three weeks ago, but nothing has happened as far as I know."

Ian says, "I'm new to this team and I don't completely understand what's happening. You say you're stepping back and wanting me to take over, but you jump in and respond every time an email is sent about this task. I just assumed you were going to continue to lead the initiative until I heard otherwise."

"I'm surprised to hear this," Jim responds. "I assumed you would come back to me with your ideas about how to implement the concept."

As the facilitator, you step in at this point because you can see what's happening: this dynamic is quickly becoming the group's *emergent* agenda.

You say, "I want to pause here for a moment. It seems that there is an opportunity to explore some assumptions that are sitting underneath the process workflow as a way to more fully understand what might be getting in your way. It's possible that the workflow is fine, but that the challenge lies in some assumptions around communication. If we decide to stick with this, we may not accomplish our original purpose, but it feels like this is important. What does the group think?"

The group decides to stick with and explore the new emergent agenda. And through that conversation, a new, deeper level of group dynamics is revealed. It turns out, Jim's style of communication feels very demanding on the rest of the team. They don't feel like he is open to questions about the work after he asks someone else to do it. This is not Jim's intention, but it is still the impact that he's having on the team.

As facilitator, you name this dynamic and ask the group to start developing awareness around moments when they are making assumptions about Jim's intentions. You encourage them to inquire of him directly, instead. Through this conversation, you have helped the group identify a larger ***developmental*** agenda: understanding intent and impact in team communications. The issues related to this developmental agenda will not be solved in one workshop. Rather, the team will need to attend to it over time and possibly work through the process with someone who can step into the role of team coach.

By preparing yourself to look for, identify, and name the different levels of group agendas in the room, you are taking the first step toward being able to consciously read the room. Armed with the ability to support a group in having meaningful, authentic, and thought-provoking conversations, you will help foster shared understanding, new thinking, and alignment on a forward direction.

HOLD THE GROUP'S AGENDA, NOT YOUR OWN

When you work with a group, it's helpful to know where they want to go. Knowing their presenting agenda enables you to hold their desired outcome—what they *hope* to achieve from working together—and more fully comprehend what else is happening in the room. Because along their journey, groups can get in their own way, and it can get especially complicated as a facilitator when what the group *thinks* they need and what they *actually* need are two different things.

In principle, we would all like for a group's relationship to their outcomes to look like the first diagram below. A nice, neat, orderly flow of collaborative processes that lead to the desired outcome. Often, however, it does *not* go this way. And when a facilitator holds tightly to the idea that this is how a meeting or meetings *should* go—when a "win" to them looks like moving the team along as quickly as possible toward the specified outcomes—it can lead them to overly drive the presenting agenda. The facilitator will, in essence, have turned the presenting agenda into their *own* agenda, and they will likely miss what else is happening in the room.

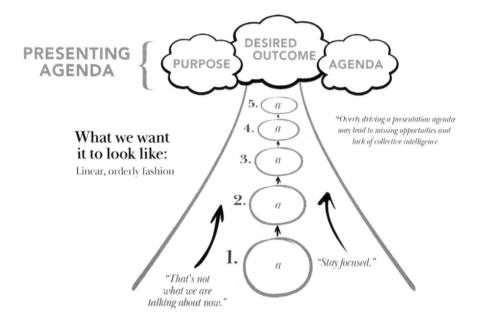

Real life is never this neat and orderly. The real path will look way more messy. It will not be linear. Sometimes, it meanders backward in order to go forward. It sometimes feels like stagnation. But these moments are when emergent and developmental group agendas come forward. These "detours" are what help a group develop and begin to see how they can improve their effectiveness.

Unexpected directions ultimately lead to better outcomes because new levels of shared understanding and clearer thinking emerge.

If we, as facilitators, drive the meeting toward the presenting agenda, we miss the emerging or developmental agendas that surface along the way.

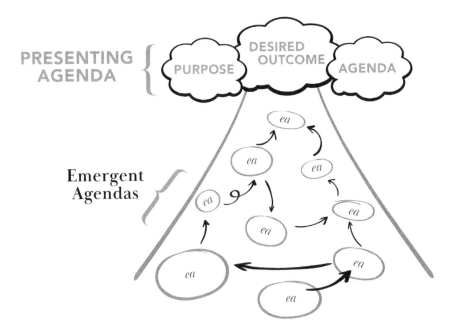

When you hold the group's agenda—presenting, emergent, or developmental—you are choosing to be of service to the group over yourself, your position, and your perception of your own worth. This is about them, not you.

The principle of holding the group's agenda is about being aware of what the group wants and how they also might be getting in their own way. It's about being able to really listen to what's emerging in the team—hearing what the team needs—while remaining aware of what your own agenda might be and not letting it take over.

Here are some examples of what emergent agendas might look like in a meeting:

- *You notice that one team member is resisting the decision-making process because she's worried about the direction the team is going and wants to prevent them from making the wrong decision.*
- *You notice that another team member may feel like no one is listening to what they say and they are disengaging from the process.*
- *You're hearing that one of the key stakeholders in the project is trying to fit more work into a shrinking time box.*
- *You notice that you are starting to dig in your heels about wanting to help the team make a final decision before the meeting ends.*

When you are equipped to help a group navigate both the presenting agenda that gives context and purpose to their time together *and* the structural patterns of group dynamics that create an emerging agenda, you will be seeing (and helping the group see) the larger developmental agenda that is afoot for them. And facilitators who are able to surface and name aspects of group and team development will be serving the group well beyond the meeting. Why? Because developmental agendas address patterns in groups that get in the way of effectiveness over the long haul.

A developmental agenda will encourage, for example:

- *Group members being able to say what they really think*
- *Group members bringing their conflict into the room and talking about it rather than having the real conversation outside the room*
- *Group members deciding on an overall direction and fully committing to it*

- *Group members welcoming different points of view*
- *Group members growing their ability to slow down enough to hear all voices*
- *Group members adopting the agile values and principles without having to question them at every step*

Your gift will be seeing the whole system, which includes how the group dynamics and invisible patterns are getting in the way. By holding the three levels of group agendas, you will be able to see well beyond today to all the possibilities in the future. You will be able to see that if this team is willing to take on the work of the developmental agenda, their presenting agendas will become more clear and more easily attainable.

HOW TO REALLY LISTEN FOR THE EMERGENT AGENDA

Many years ago I was working with a leadership team who had been trying to define common goals—things they could be in alignment on rather than separated and divided by. Their *presenting* agenda was that they wanted more alignment and to be a team. So far so good. In fact, their goal was highly aligned with my *own* beliefs about what makes leadership teams effective: having alignment around shared goals and functioning as a team. And, since it came from them, it was *their* agenda! Great!

But my love for their agenda clouded my vision to the reality of what was playing out in their conversations every time they began to talk about the topic on the table. During a two-day offsite, the team got really bogged down in their conversation and just seemed to be going nowhere. Every facilitation move I made just created more directionless spin. There was deep resistance, yet I kept pushing the conversation forward.

113

After a while, we took a break. I remember feeling so frustrated by not being able to figure out what was wrong. I was frustrated by the lack of progress the group was making and was even becoming ambivalent about my work with them. I felt like I was letting them down and failing as a facilitator. Why was it so difficult to come around to a decision?

And then it hit me. I was holding tightly to their presenting agenda—and, sneakily, it had become *my* agenda, too. But if I really listened to their conversation, I could hear that they did not actually want to be aligned around common goals. The words they used, the resistance to moving to closure on a decision, the constant swirl in the conversations—these are all the hallmarks of an emerging agenda.

When we reconvened after the break, I stated what I was seeing. "You've been talking about this topic for some time now," I said. "I hear you repeatedly articulating that you want to align around common goals, but what plays out in your conversations is the opposite. You resist the idea. I've come to believe that I want alignment for you more than you want it for yourselves, and that's not a good place to be. I can't want it more than you do."

If I had kept to the path that this leadership team was on, the group would have continued to lack energy and commitment. In fact, I don't believe the group would have ever come to a consensus decision about what to do. If I had not caught sight of the fact that my own agenda had become so tightly tied to their presenting agenda that I was missing the more emergent and developmental agendas, one of two things would likely have happened:

- *We would have just continued to spin forever*
- *The group might have blamed me for failing to help them meet their goals*

Instead, we had a conversation about what it was like for them to want something in principle but, in practice, feel unwilling to let go of the way they were currently working. We decided to park the topic of alignment for a later date, agreeing that they were not collectively ready for it just yet. The tension was named, and the group made an intentional decision that created a huge sense of relief—both the group and for me. We were no longer fighting the resistance.

So, what was their emergent agenda? It was to let go of (and to make an intentional decision to stop) pursuing something that they didn't really want at that moment. It was to free themselves to focus their energy on other areas.

Agendas are tricky. Your job is to be on the lookout for them. The feel of resistance, or when something begins to feel hard, or like you're doing all the work, or like you're dragging a boulder up a hill...these are all good indicators to stop and take a wider-systems view. Name what's happening or what you're experiencing, and ask the group what they're experiencing. Sometimes what a group thinks they want is not what they're ready for. When the actions don't match the words, help the group see that in a morally neutral way—without judgement or making them wrong.

GO SLOW TO GO FAST

The slippery slope with agendas is that when your own agenda feels *so right* to you, you risk missing the group's agenda. And if you're facilitating a team in which you are a member of the team, discerning your agenda from the team's agenda becomes even more difficult.

I once watched an agile facilitator cling so tightly to his own agenda over the course of a meeting that he made a lasting negative impact. He was determined to get his team through a decision regarding the next release. He was pretty familiar with the features that were on the table, and he had a pretty good idea of what should be selected and why. So, when he brought the team together for release planning, he occasionally inserted his opinion about the content.

Over the course of the process, some team members began to debate with the facilitator, arguing about why a feature should or should not be included. Meanwhile, several of the team members became withdrawn and silent. This dynamic caused the facilitator to push even harder for a decision, since he knew that the team was under a tight deadline and needed to reach a decision. Only later did the facilitator discover that part of the group's hesitation related to a technical issue that had recently emerged. It would have impacted their decision, but the lead architect didn't feel like he was being heard in the conversation and had decided to withdraw from the debate.

At the end of the day, the meeting ended with no decision—just a team of people who were very frustrated with the facilitator. In fact, they no longer trusted him.

This facilitator had been in high-stakes mode. He was scared that the team's inability to make a decision quickly was a reflection on *his* value and worth as a facilitator. He started to doubt that the team had the knowledge to make the decision, and he began contributing content and letting his own, fear-based agenda drive his choices in the moment.

He had stepped fully out of the principles of facilitation.

Over the next few months, this pattern continued. Eventually, the architect withdrew from the conversations altogether. He came to the meetings and followed directions, but he was unwilling to make the effort to contribute. The facilitator began to make assumptions about the architect: "he's just like that," "he's always derailing the conversations," "he just doesn't get it." As a result, the facilitator continued to just ignore the architect, believing that the team was much more efficient when they simply factored out his voice.

Unfortunately (and unsurprisingly), the price was paid in the team's design decisions, and a significant amount of rework was required.

So, what could this facilitator have done differently to stay in integrity with the group's agenda?

In that pivotal meeting moment when people went silent, there was a choice to make. Instead of plowing ahead toward a decision, the facilitator could have slowed down long enough to see what was happening. He could have named it for the group and asked about it. He could have said, "Let's pause here for a moment. I'm noticing several people have gone silent. What's happening for you right now?"

By inquiring about what was happening, the facilitator would have been choosing to engage in a conversation squarely within the emerging agenda. It may have taken a few minutes to *have* that conversation, but it would have saved the team months of disengagement, frustration, and reworking.

Sometimes, the efficient choice is simply to slow down. Teams are often under a great deal of pressure to do work efficiently—twice the work in half the time. This pressure, either self-imposed or imposed from the outside, creates a tension in teams. They feel like they need to "get it done" just as quickly as possible in order to move onto the next step. But humans don't always work that way. There are very few black-and-white, right-or-wrong decisions these days. Our work and team environments are complex systems with lots of moving pieces and parts. There might not be a clear right or wrong, but making intentional choices with clarity about the potential impacts can support teams in moving forward.

What gets in the way of efficiency and effectiveness is plowing through conversations. It's trampling on others and leaving them in your wake. How fast a team moves along their agile journey or through to a productive outcome is not necessarily a reflection on your worth and skill as an agile facilitator. Sometimes the greater path to efficiency is to take the pause. To slow down the action in order to gain the momentum. To go deeper before you go forward. To look back and repair broken trust before you look forward again. To address the emergent agenda.

It's a dance, and sometimes the action to take is the thing that feels counter-productive in the moment.

Holding vs. not holding the group's agenda—what it looks and feels like for facilitators

HOLDING THE GROUP'S AGENDA

Internal assumptions and beliefs	• This is *their* agenda
	• Agendas are emergent and can change
	• Resistance is not dysfunctional, it's an indicator that something is missing or needed
	• Inability to converge or decide may mean there is something that still needs to be discussed
Behaviors	• Asking, "'How can I best serve this group?"
	• Asking, "What's needed now?"
	• Treating all the group's actions as data about what they really need
	• Meeting resistance with curiosity
	• Being aware of the difference between the facilitator's desire and the group's needs
	• Creating a space that allows for opposition to both process and content
	• Normalizing opposition by calling for it and asking about red flags
	• Owning the process and being open to feedback about it (without jumping to change the process too quickly)

NOT HOLDING THE GROUP'S AGENDA
(i.e., driving YOUR agenda)

Internal assumptions and beliefs	• They don't know where they need to go, but I do
	• I can see all the possibilities for this group, they just can't follow along
	• I am valuable to this group if I design a perfect group process
	• If we don't achieve the stated outcomes, I will have failed as facilitator
	• The failure of this process could lead to getting fired
	• If I change the design of the process, all that time will be wasted
Behaviors	• Pushing the group through the plan, even though you're getting resistance
	• Colluding with others' agendas
	• Using the authority of your role as facilitator to take charge or influence the group
	• Not having a clear purpose for the meeting and/or not radiating it

WATCH OUT FOR COLLUSION AND INDIVIDUAL AGENDAS

There is power in the role of facilitator. You hold the group process. It's easy for team members, leaders, and external stakeholders to get lured into thinking that if they just have an offline conversation with you—if they just explain what's going on from their perspective—then you'll be able to help them solve a problem or guide a group in a certain direction.

These requests are a great example of individual agendas. They are not the group's agenda.

Often, I encounter requests like this when the individual making it does not feel like they can voice their concern to the group. In moments like this, there is a choice for you as the facilitator. You can collude with the individuals and keep the secret, or you can let the moment inform how you work with the group as whole. If you feel like you've been asked to keep a secret or hold someone's personal agenda, help them understand what the role of a facilitator is. The best course of action is to then ask what would need to be true in order for them to bring their request or concern to the group rather than to you.

When efforts to engage you in offline conversation happen, recognize that they are serving a purpose: they are an indicator that something is needed or missing, and they bring the subterranean group dynamics you might not see on the surface right to the very top.

If your scope in the process is a basic level of facilitation, you might check in with the group and inquire about how it's going. You could ask questions like, "Are we making progress?" or, "Is there anything we need to talk about that we're not talking about already?" You might ask the group to write things down, or you could put them in breakout groups and ask them to pull themes forward. Once you have more information, you can design a group process that will help more voices come forward.

If you're working at a more advanced level of facilitation, you might also name the pattern of communication you are noticing in the group and inquire about it. You might even design a process to *change* the pattern. Or, if you've contracted to both facilitate and coach the team, you might pause the group process altogether and ask the group to reflect on how they are working together.

However deep you go, these are all different ways of holding the group's agenda. You are taking what you see back to the group and intervening in the process so they can move forward more productively.

When holding the group's agenda, remember to let individual voices dictate your *curiosity*, not your decisions. Requests for "secret keeping" (offline conversations with the facilitator) are not only unhelpful and unproductive, they will get you into a mess. Just don't do it. When facilitation becomes a role for influencing or manipulation, the group will not trust the process and group effectiveness will be impacted.

STARTING THE PRACTICE

Agendas emerge. They ebb and flow like the tide. Sometimes, through interviews and data collection, you might be able to identify both the presenting agenda and a possible emergent agenda ahead of a meeting. Other times, emergent and developmental agendas will surface through conversations in the meeting itself. If you're working with a team for only one or two meetings, it might make sense to hold tighter to the outcome. But if your overall objective is to help the team develop, then sticking to the presenting agenda at every meeting will likely cause you to miss great opportunities!

One of your primary jobs as a facilitator, therefore, is to listen. *Really* listen. If you evaluate your facilitation practice solely on achieving the desired outcome of the meeting every time, you might be missing bigger, more impactful issues.

The following practices will help guide you as you begin to discern the different types of agendas you'll encounter in the room—presenting, emergent, and developmental. The presenting agenda can sometimes just represent the safe, "acceptable" topic. The *real* topic might be much riskier and not safe to name. It is likely to emerge when we least expect it—when meetings become "rote" or when we feel like we're just going through the motions without actually listening to what's said. While it might feel like something's not relevant in the moment, chances are that it represents an unspoken, "undercover" agenda, and it could be the key to unlocking new levels of connection, collaboration, thinking, innovation, and team performance.

Lesson 1: Be as mindful as possible

How you show up in the room is more impactful than the group processes you have in your toolkit. I'm a recovering tool seeker, so this lesson has taken years for me to fully absorb. It's not that you don't need to have a full toolkit for working with group process, it's that how you show up—how you *engage*—is what has the most powerful impact in any given room. So bring the processes, and then bring your best self!

Here are five core practices (and some questions to ask yourself) that will serve you well in holding the agenda:

- *Be your best self*
- *Who are you being when you are at your best?*
- *How can you best serve this team today?*
- *Listen*
- *What's really being said in the meeting?*
- *What's not being said?*
- *What themes do you hear?*
- *Be aware of your own agenda.*
- *What is your agenda?*
- *Are you willing to set your agenda aside today?*
- *What will help you let it go?*
- *What part of your agenda might conflict with the group's agenda?*
- *Be curious*
- *What's happening in the moment?*
- *What's changed?*
- *What might be emerging next?*
- *Co-facilitate*

◆ *If you're aware that you have a strong agenda, is there a colleague who can co-facilitate with you?*

◆ *What feedback can they give you after?*

Lesson 2: Collect data in advance

The first step to holding the group's agenda is understanding what's present in the team. Since agendas are created from the collective voice of the group, the best way to do this is by collecting input from the meeting sponsor and from the group itself prior to the meeting. Conducting interviews or surveying the participants ahead of the meeting is a good way to do it. They help you hear the unbiased views of each person before you ever set foot in the room. In fact, I recommend just making surveys and/or interviews a part of your Planning and Design for Facilitation process whenever possible, especially if the topic has a high degree of complexity.

Surveys

Surveys are a great way to collect data and ask quantifiable questions that can be shared back with the group in the form of charts and graphs. It's also helpful if you don't have a lot of time or have a large group that you need input from. Surveys are your opportunity to ask each of the participants what *they* think the presenting agenda should tackle.

Interviews

If you have time and the topic calls for it, interviews are helpful because they provide a way for you to hear the narrative and thinking behind why team members are feeling the way they do. It allows you to inquire more deeply into what's happening on the team. Developing interview questions based on how the general survey was answered also provides a way to be more targeted with your inquiry.

You might ask questions like:

- *What do you see happening in this team?*
- *What's missing?*
- *Where does the team get stuck?*
- *How do you feel about _____ (project, decision, direction)?*
- *What is your biggest concern?*

Interviews and surveys are more effective if you agree upfront with the participants that you will maintain their anonymity and that you will only share the results at a thematic level. You are not on a witch hunt to point fingers, blame, or accuse. You are curious about what people think, about what they would say to you one on one. You want to know what they don't feel comfortable sharing in the large group and what it is that's holding them back. If you are a team member or leader in addition to being the facilitator and you worry that people might not be as candid and forthright with you, then consider asking a colleague or external facilitator to conduct the survey and interviews.

Once you have gathered the data, look for themes. What did you hear more than once from more than one person? Make sure to phrase the themes you see in your own words. You have promised anonymity, so this will help build trust.

And finally, it's time for you to decide how you will help the participants see their emergent agenda—the group dynamic that's getting in the way of moving through the presenting agenda and decision process.

- *When you collect data, how will you share it with them?*
- *Collecting data about a team changes the power dynamics between you and them. You now know information that they do*

not have. So, it's important to think of ways you can share it
back with them in a way that remains neutral and anonymous.
Some ways to do this are:

- *Sharing data and graphs*
- *Capturing the themes from the interviews and sharing*
  them ahead of time
- *Sharing the interview themes during the meeting itself*
- *Help the team process the data*
- *There is nothing more frustrating to a team than taking*
  the time to give input or feedback and then notice that
  nothing is really done with the data. Collecting data is
  not the point. What matters most when working with
  a team is that they are given an opportunity to make
  meaning and sense of the data collected. They need time
  to talk about it so they can come to a shared understand-
  ing of what the data is trying to show them.

Lesson 3: Help the group surface
their agendas in the room

Sometimes the greatest way a facilitator can be of service to a
team is to disregard any meeting agenda or timebox they had and
just name what's really happening in the room. By doing so, the
facilitator is surfacing the tension that might exist from different
agendas or from misalignment.

On one team, I watched members struggle with the idea of even
being a team. They were resistant to activities that had them work
on team agreements or that sought to help them come to alignment on their purpose and objectives. The facilitator finally named
the tension, saying, "It seems to me there are at least two different
agendas in the room. This first is that you are a group of people
who need to function as a team. The other is that there is no reason
for this group to even *be* a team. What do others see? How does

this unresolved issue get in your way?" From that point forward, the facilitator's statement and subsequent questions became the sole focus of the meeting.

This situation was a perfect example of an **observation-question prompt,** which is a powerful way to help a group surface competing agendas.

The point of an observation-question prompt is to notice something about the group's work or conversation in a neutral, non-judging tone. Then simply ask about it:

- *"You seem stuck. What's stuck?"*
- *"We have a Move to go in this direction and a Move to go in another direction. Which one would serve you best to do first?"*

You have seen examples of this phrasing throughout this book, and it really works. When a group feels stuck in some way, be curious. Reframe conflict and tension as behavior that is trying to be helpful rather than treating them as something derailing or disrupting.

Trying to push through resistance by ignoring it or asking people to save their concerns for another time can cause the group to entrench further. Instead, help the group surface the issue by simply naming it and asking, "What would be useful to this group right now?"

Lesson 4: Find your "no"

> "Only once you give yourself permission to stop trying to do it all, to stop saying yes to everyone, can you make your highest contribution toward the things that really matter."
> ~Greg McKeown, author of *Essentialism: The Disciplined Pursuit of Less*

Finding your "no" is difficult. It's something you may struggle with throughout your career. But it's critical, because not every group, team, meeting purpose, or desired outcome is for you. Just because a team has an agenda and an outcome that they want to achieve does not mean that it's a good fit for how *you* think and work with groups.

One example of a good time to use your "no" is when you can tell that you will not be able to hold the group's agenda.

Very early on in my facilitation career, I was asked to facilitate a group toward a *predetermined* outcome. The meeting sponsor had already decided what outcome he wanted, and my job was to help the group see it as *their* decision. While the meeting didn't blow up, it also didn't go well. I suspect the group was used to this sort of coercive behavior from their meeting sponsor.

That was the first and last time I ever accepted a facilitation opportunity like that. Facilitating a group toward a predetermined outcome is not the purpose of facilitation, and it's not an agenda I can hold. To put it another way, asking a group to participate in a process where the outcome has already been decided by others is not collaboration, and you are not facilitating.

Although never simple, the answer when asked to "facilitate" in a situation like this is to politely decline the facilitation role.

Of course, it is easier to say "no" if you are an external facilitator. If you are an internal facilitator, it might feel much more challenging. If you feel out of alignment with the group's agenda, chances are there are some bigger issues at play in the organization. It may feel risky to your career to push back so strongly on something you are being asked to do. In this case, the task may be to reframe your pushback (your "no") through the lens of curiosity. Rather than digging in and saying "this isn't for me," consider how you can help the sponsor see what you are seeing.

Let's go back to my anecdote above, where the sponsor asked me to coerce the group into a decision that had already been made. Instead of saying "no, I think this is not for me," what if I had engaged in a candid conversation with the sponsor about the impact of asking a team to participate in this sort of collaboration theater? Here's what I could have said:

> "It sounds like you are pretty clear on the decision and direction you want to head. I also hear you wanting to value the input of the group and getting their perspective. I'm not willing to design a collaborative process for a group on a decision that's already been made—that would be a waste of their time and likely very frustrating to them and you. What I would suggest instead is you present the decision that's been made, and we then use the time to have the group identify the risks and opportunities that the decision might create. They can help collectively create a set of actions for implementation."

In this hypothetical, I would have been finding my way around a specific part of the request while using my knowledge of how collaboration and teams work best to provide an alternative proposal for helping the sponsor get at what they really wanted. This kind of conversation would be important for either an internal or external facilitator to have when a scenario doesn't feel right, but as an *internal* facilitator, this is a way to think about changing the conversation when you might feel like you have fewer options.

You owe it to yourself and the team to challenge the notion of certain agendas.

A practice I have today is to spend more time before a collaborative meeting helping people decide what degree of collaboration is needed and what the purpose or outcome of the meeting really is. This builds directly on the practices learned in the last chapter, as well. The goal is to determine when to involve a group in an open collaborative process and when it's more appropriate to just make a clear decision and inform the group. To my mind, part of the art of holding the group's agenda is understanding when—or if—facilitation even has a role in the process, as well as what part of the process you will actually be facilitating.

The lesson here is to ask yourself: what are *your* boundaries? When would you politely decline to facilitate a group, or how would you reframe the engagement?

CONCLUSION

I want to leave you with a few key thoughts. Holding the Group's Agenda is big work, and some of the more important work you can do with a team as they develop. In *The Advantage*, Patrick Lencioni notes that "there is no better way to have a fundamental impact on an organization than by changing the way it does meetings."[10] The way to change meetings is to help teams and groups move the meeting from a surface-level conversation where they may as well be rearranging the deck chairs on the Titanic to a place where it's okay and even expected to have *real* conversations. Conversations that are emergent, that name difficult topics, that create space for different thinking, and where new thinking happens. Most groups need guidance and help getting to this place, and the organization's culture and team dynamics will have a big impact on how easy the process is. But

---

10   Patrick Lencioni, *The Advantage: Why Organizational Health Trumps Everything in Business* (San Francisco: Jossey-Bass, 2012), 173.

this is the work to do. Without it, you're wasting time—yours and everyone else's.

Don't sit idly by and claim that this work is too hard, or not safe. Don't wring your hands with fear over what might happen. Instead, pick your head up and look toward the future. What's one small step today that this group can take toward having the real conversation? What's one small thing that you can do to bring more safety to the situation? What's one way you can reframe the conversation to make it more meaningful? What is this team avoiding? What might *you* be avoiding?

Don't shy away from emergent and developmental agendas, even when it's tough. This work lays the track for agile teams to become agile, and each meeting is a meaningful step toward more systemic change within the team or organizational culture.

CHAPTER 5:

Upholding the Agile Mindset

Upholding the agile mindset is the fifth principle of the Agile Team Facilitation Stance. It is specific to teams who are seeking agility in their work, meaning that they want to be adaptable to change, that they believe small chunks of work provide value, that they focus on the customer first, and that they are committed to collaborating with others.

This chapter is for you if you are in some way charged with the responsibility of helping a team become agile. My intention is to offer you a way forward in helping a team adopt agility without telling them what to do. In its most basic form, this means leaning into a new way of leading that is more facilitative than directive.

If you are in the agile world, know that teams need both your expertise in agility to help them close knowledge gaps around creating flow in their work *and* they need you to create the environment and conditions that support true collaboration. This is where facilitating a team and coaching a team start to meet. In team coaching, we want to build the team's ability to do their own work. In facilitation, which is the focus of this book, we are focused on moving the team toward an outcome while helping them uphold the agile mindset.

Responding to a common struggle among new facilitators, this chapter is about how to bridge the need for your expertise in agility and the need for true collaboration. But if you are not in the world of agility, don't worry. This chapter will help deepen your ability to identify when you're bringing your own point of view into the conversation, and it will develop your ability to navigate your opinions while maintaining neutrality.

WHAT DOES IT MEAN TO FACILITATE WHILE UPHOLDING THE AGILE MINDSET?

All facilitators, not just agile facilitators, will find themselves better equipped to create space for collaboration and communication by staying grounded in the first four Agile Team Facilitation Stance principles (Maintaining Neutrality, Standing in the Storm, Honoring the Wisdom of the Group, and Holding the Group's Agenda). What makes agile facilitation unique is not the *skills* of facilitation it requires. What sets you apart as an *agile* facilitator is the unique position you hold as a part of the team.

You are a part of the team, but when you are facilitating, your role is to stand apart from the team. And you will find that upholding the agile mindset is the part of the facilitation stance that is not about pure facilitation. Most significantly, this is the part where you, as a facilitator, have an opinion or point of view about how something can be done.

This dualism causes tension for many new facilitators. You may feel a deep stake in the outcome of the decision being made in the room, and you may feel like you will be held personally accountable if the team makes the "wrong" decision.

> The principle of upholding the agile mindset helps build a firm foundation for succeeding in this tricky—but essential—role.

First off, it's important to acknowledge that if you are standing solidly in the other four principles of facilitation, you'll be just fine—even if you don't uphold the mindset of agility. You are still facilitating, you just won't be supporting *agility*.

Upholding the agile mindset means acknowledging that you are the model for agility in the room. You model it in the way you interact with the team, the way you adapt to things in the moment, and the way you help the team focus. You lead with servant leadership, always asking how you can support the team as you guide them toward the highest and best use of their time together.

Upholding the agile mindset also means that, as facilitator, it is your job to help the *team* uphold the agile mindset. For example, if a team member decides they no longer want to be part of collaborative meetings—that they just want to go off and do their assigned work on their own—your job is not to tell them they are wrong and that they must come to the meeting anyway because it's agile. Your role as a facilitator is to be curious. Inquire about where this viewpoint comes from and what would need to be true in order for this person to be willing to collaborate. By remaining curious and in the conversation, you are now modeling in a very meta way what it means to be collaborative.

Remember: you are not truly being agile if you are not collaborating and communicating effectively, and collaboration and effective communication takes facilitation. That's the foundational belief you carry when you step into the role of facilitator. It stands to reason, then, that if you carry this belief with you into your practice in the room, chances are good that you are upholding the agile mindset.

THE AGILE MINDSET ≠ TOOLS AND PRACTICES

Facilitating while upholding the agile mindset starts with one simple premise:

> You are the guardian of the values and principles of the agile mindset, not the adjudicator of the agile practices.

Confusion around this point can create a "bad taste" for some teams and organizations around the concept of agility itself. One team I worked with, for example, was adamant that they never wanted to hear the word "agile" again. Of course, when I hear something along these lines, I always get really curious. What story sits behind those strong feelings? For this team, it was that they had once worked with an agile coach who spent the whole time telling them what to do because, he said, that's what Scrum is about! The coach talked to the team like they didn't know how to do their work. He asked questions, but did not really listen to their answers. It didn't work for them. As a result, the team told me, they "operate in an agile way," but they "do it differently than the coach wanted."

Telling people what to do, forcing process, or not listening to what's happening on the team is *not* what upholding the agile mindset is about. Yet, time and time again, we see new facilitators conflating the agile mindset with the *tools* that they use to facilitate.

Let's explore this confusion through the lens of retrospectives. These are one of the practices that I see teams grow weary of very quickly.

Initially, when a team is just starting to use retros, the process will often feel fresh, unique, maybe even transformative in nature. But, over time, teams frequently find that they don't want to do them anymore. Or they find that scheduling a one-hour retro is a waste of time and agree to schedule them quarterly, instead. Maybe they even decide to go offsite for the day when the time comes.

There are several common complaints that emerge when teams gather for retrospectives:

- *"We don't have time. The next stage of this project starts soon, and we don't have time to carve out an hour—much less a day—to do a retro."*
- *"The questions of 'what worked?' 'what didn't work?' and 'what would you do differently?' have become trite and overused."*
- *"The process of always using stickies and dots to vote on items keeps the conversation at the surface level."*

Upholding the agile mindset does *not* look like defending the use of retrospectives as a tried-and-true method of starting conversations. Instead, it means asking the group questions like:

- *What's working about the process?*
- *How can we make the process different?*
- *What would need to be true in order for you to get value out of this tool?*

At some point, you might find that the team stops finding value even in *questions* about retrospectives. They may actually want to explore different kinds of questions altogether. Questions like:

- *What's it like to be on this team?*
- *What are some ways that we exclude people or ideas in our team?*
- *How might we solve some of our complex issues differently?*

These are not the standard retrospective questions, and that's good! Upholding the agile mindset means helping the team evolve the practices. Ultimately, the goal is to help them create their own practices and tools while still upholding the principles of agility.

AGILE ADAPTABILITY

It's easy to fall into the trap of becoming the "practice police." This is when you think it's your job to ensure the team follows a specific practice, just as it's written. But upholding the agile mindset means becoming the "guardian of the values and principles," instead.

When you reach the point where you find yourself—and possibly the team—getting bored, you may no longer be producing the results you had hoped for. Especially when you first start upholding the agile mindset, you might find yourself leaning more heavily on practices in a particular agile framework (e.g., Scrum, Kanban, SaFE, etc.), and that's okay! We have to start somewhere and so does the team. These practices exist to help us make actionable meaning of what values and principles might look like. So, find inspiration in the practices that others have created and try them out.

But when you find your team moving through the questions identified in the section above, you'll know it's time to move on. It's time to let the team adapt the practices while helping them keep to the values.

For many facilitators who reach this point, the concern becomes whether they might "break agile" by trying something new. You won't. In part, your job as a facilitator is to help teams adapt by inventing their *own* framework for agility. It will transcend and include everything they've done before, but it will be their own.

David Kantor talks about the process of model building in *Reading the Room*. He observes that we all model build. When we learn a new process, theory, or skill set, we imitate first, then we feel constrained, and finally we create something new. We make it our own!

Let's break it down:

- **Imitation**
  We follow others and do what they do. Imitation is our way of getting started. It's why we look for mentors and others who we can emulate.

- **Constraint**
  Eventually, we will start to strain against the model. We'll push back and oppose certain parts of it. "Keep this, not that" will become a part of our inner dialogue.

♦ **Autonomy**

This is the space of creating something new. This is where our own model starts to emerge. Autonomy comes from experience, practice, learning, and feedback.

In agility, teams and organizations too often get stuck at imitation. We take on practices that have been defined in a framework or playbook by someone else, but we hesitate or stop altogether when we feel called to recalibrate.

As a team matures, it's *important* for them to push on these practices—to challenge them, shape them, expand them. If the practices don't ever change, then people check out of the process. If they don't find value in the tool or practice, then they don't want to do it. In sense, it's the very essence of becoming rigid and less agile.

Here's the question: can we let frameworks be our guide, not our commandments? Can we just let them serve as the foundation to help us get started, something we can imitate to get us going on our own learning journey? Then, when we're ready, can we be willing to take the bold move to create a framework that is unique to our team, our organization?

The answer is yes. And this is the shift that comes when we develop our agile facilitation skills to the point that we achieve mastery over them. Not in spite of the agile principles, but in *alignment* with them.

So keep working at it! The key is to honor the values and principles of agility without holding too tightly to how a team manifests those principles.

STARTING THE PRACTICE

Starting the practice of upholding the agile mindset means understanding the values and principles of agility. It means thinking intentionally about how you want to bring your point of view and experience forward in the group process. It means starting to recognize that you can help close a knowledge gap by offering your expertise on agility or by offering your experience of what it feels like in the moment when the principles of agility are (or are not) valued.

Ultimately, focusing on upholding the agile mindset means learning how to bridge the divide between principles and practices. It's about what we do in the moment. As facilitator, you're the one who is able to help a team see where they might be living into the agile values—and where they might *not* be.

Lesson 1: Develop a deep understanding of the agile practices and mindset

Upholding the agile mindset is not just about knowing how to do a practice (e.g., knowing the three questions to ask during a standup), it's about knowing *why* you would use this practice in the first place:

* *What's the purpose of the practice?*
* *How does it bring agility to a team?*
* *Why would they do it?*
* *What ways might they adapt the practice and still hold to the principles?*

This grounding—this sense of *why* we do what we do—will help you ask the right questions and develop effective ways to tailor the practices later on.

You may have noticed that there is emerging thinking in approaches like Joshua Kerievsky's Modern Agile and Alistair Cockburn's Heart of Agile that offer new thought leadership around the agile values and principles. There is also a whole universe of agile frameworks like Scrum, Extreme Programming, Kanban, SaFE, Scaled Agile, etc., that define and describe agile practices and roles. These frameworks emerged as a way to make sense of and make actionable the values and principles first identified in the Agile Manifesto.

There are lots of debates about which of these frameworks is better, which one is "more agile," but what's important from a facilitation perspective is that you know what the team or organization is using. You need to be very familiar with the practices—enough that you know how work flows, why the practices exist in the manner they do, what principles and values the practices express—and you need to be clear about how you might adapt the practice but still hold to the core values and principles.

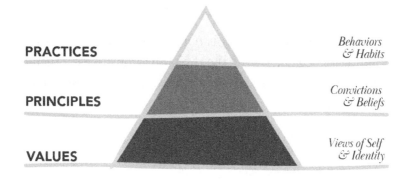

Lesson 2: Assess how agile the team is and ask, "Am I the right facilitator?"

When you engage with a team, it's helpful to ask yourself a few questions:

- *Where is this team in their agility mindset?*
- *How mature is this team in their practice of agility?*

Teams that are just getting started with agility need more education and more structure to their practices. Teams that have been doing this for a while and have some knowledge under their belt need less structure and education. They need more neutral facilitation.

Understanding where the team is at is your first step in understanding how to navigate your role as the facilitator. And a helpful way to assess the team's agile practice is to ask them questions during the Design and Planning phase of your facilitation preparation:

- *How long have you been working with or toward an agile mindset?*
- *What are the areas where you feel like you're doing really well?*
- *Where would you like to improve?*
- *What would improvement look like to you?*

There are also formal agility assessments and surveys that take a more holistic view of agility, any one of which can help a team make sense of where they stand. However you choose to make the assessment, just remember to include the team in the conversation rather than having their agility be diagnosed by leaders or other stakeholders outside the team. Let the team have a voice and a say in the focus of their work.

Once you've assessed the team's experience with agility, pause. Then decide whether you are actually the right facilitator for this team:

- *What stage of team development is this group in?*
- *What do they need from you as their facilitator?*

Upholding the agile mindset is about simultaneously understanding where **you** are at and understanding where the **group** is at.

If you are mature in your practice of agility and the team is not, your work will be to meet them where they are. If, however, a team is mature in their agile mindset and practice but you are just starting out, you might not be the best facilitator for that team. What do you do? When you critically assess the situation and discover that you may not be the right facilitator, it can feel uncomfortable—especially when that's the role you have been assigned. If you feel there is a gap, figure out how you might close the gap for yourself. Work with a mentor who is masterful in agility. Bring in a co-facilitator who can co-design facilitated sessions with you. Create your own plan for how you will support the team in meeting them where they are. Many of the practices discussed in this book can be adapted to support you through the process of developing your understanding of agility.

Lesson 3: Uncover the key for upholding agility with this particular team

As you help a team find their agile foundation, you will want to help them focus on the value or principle of agility that will have the most impact. Include them in the process of defining their agile focus! You might invite the team to have a conversation about all the agile principles and then select one or two that they want to work on first.

Try asking questions like:

- *What's one agile value or principle that will have the most impact on our work right now?*
- *How do we want to approach incorporating this value or principle into our work?*

Uncovering the agile value or principle that will have the most impact on how the team works together is like finding the right key for a lock. It empowers the team to make choices about their own effectiveness and helps them learn to have conversations about how they *work*, not just about what they do.

One of the biggest sources of resistance when it comes to agile practices is when a team feels like agile is being "done to them" rather than having some say in what happens. This is a great reason to include a team in the decision-making around what to focus on. But the trick is to be prepared. Make sure that you've already spent the time developing a deep understanding of agility to ensure that you can really help them once you've collaboratively determined which agile principle will help move the team forward in the moment.

Lesson 4: Provide process, not solutions

Remember in *The Karate Kid* when Daniel wanted to learn to fight? Mr. Miyagi didn't just *tell* Daniel what to do. He helped him develop different practices outside the context of a fight. Each new practice created new muscle memories, and when it was time to step into the ring during the final competition, Daniel had everything he needed to bring it all together. Daniel was able to pull on the memory of each individual practice, in his own way and in real time.

Mr. Miyagi's approach is what mastery looks like: you've done something so many times that you are able to break it down to its fundamental elements and help someone *else* learn to do the same. It's not about an end-product that looks the same for everyone, it's about learning the fundamentals so well that they can be applied effectively in any situation. This is exactly like the principles and values of agility, which a team can apply in a way that's unique to them and their needs.

Upholding the agile mindset is about **breaking agility down into tangible chunks** to help your team learn and grow. Just like Mr. Miyagi did for Daniel.

Spotify provides an awesome example of what happens when you understand a concept, values, and principles so thoroughly that you can adapt them to fit your culture and needs. Spotify took the values and principles of agility, tried them out in the context of their culture, and created their own model for what agile would look like when practiced at Spotify. Their new model consisted of squads, chapters, guilds, and tribes. It was their own model and a new way of thinking. It evolved from experiments and from learning what worked in their organization while remaining consistently focused on the customer.

But you can't take what Spotify did, put it in a document, and apply it in any other organizational culture (although many have tried). That would be like copying everything Daniel did in his final fight—all the hand movements and that famous kick—without any of the training, muscle memory, or the "in-the-bones" understanding of why you do something the way you do it. You get none of the integration, the frustration of failing, the getting-my-butt-kicked-and-not-knowing-what-to-do-next demoralization, the experience of feeling so down that you don't know any way out. That was all *Daniel's* journey. And it was the personal learning, growth, and mindset shifts of that journey that allowed him to show up the way he did.

In other words, you can't record the final fight and just copy the moves. This is a journey of your own.

No two cultures are the same. There will never be another Spotify. No organization can look like *that* company at *that* moment in time. But you can be inspired by what they did. You can even borrow something from their model—but you have to take the time to integrate it into *your* context. This takes work. Dialogue. Failure. Willingness to learn from trying something new.

So, what's the takeaway? You need to know how *you* will apply the principles of agility. You need to know what *your* model is. And once you can do this for yourself, you can help your team do it, too. Facilitating teams toward agility means creating a container and a learning environment that supports the process of discovery and invention, that fits the culture, and that remains focused on the customer.

CONCLUSION

Upholding the agile mindset is not about convincing a team to buy into agile. It's about helping a team focus on how they work. It's about looking for ways to improve how they work so that they can be more effective, more empowered, enjoy their work, and experience better outcomes.

When you're able to do this, your approach to facilitating agility within teams may take a more agile approach. You will be willing to offer concepts to a team without being tightly tied to whether they agree; you will be able to break down the practices into smaller chunks that focus more on learning a principle than performing a practice; you will be able to help a team adopt a learning mindset and embrace failures; and you will able to offer guidance to teams navigating their own agile maturity.

Agile, as a movement, has had a profound impact on the way we work. But like any movement, it has taken a very large community with very diverse perspectives and opinions to bring it to life. It's the diversity of views that has led to the many different ways you can "be" agile. And, like any movement at scale, this diversity creates difference. Different models, thinking, frameworks, and the need to view something as "wrong" in order to make your view "right"...this has all become familiar territory. In this community, we can sometimes fall into a trap of debating with others: whose thinking or doing is "more agile"? Whose is less?

In truth, it's as simple as this: agility in action can look different. What's needed is critical reflection about how well what we're doing at any given moment lives into and upholds the core values and principles.

CHAPTER 6:

Developing and Mastering Your Facilitation Stance

In each of the preceding chapters, I shared lessons about how to start your practice. These lessons lay the foundation to support your awareness around each of the five principles of agile team facilitation, and they will help you stand strong in your facilitation stance in any context.

Yet those lessons are just the beginning of your journey as a facilitator.

Let's be frank. What's at the heart of wisdom is candor, honesty, authenticity, and vulnerability. In other words, being a real human being who is tapped into their inner wisdom. Teamwork and facilitation is not for the faint of heart. Tools, structures, agendas, and post-it notes only get you so far. We all have to do the rest, individually and together.

As a facilitator, you have to find your own source of courage. Courage to say what you see, to inquire about difficult subjects, to not walk past the elephant in the room. This chapter offers lessons that are designed to help you do this work and deepen your practice. As you develop and then master your facilitation stance, you will find that the work of self-awareness and group awareness is always ongoing. The lessons in this chapter are designed to support you throughout your career, deepening your skillset to help groups communicate and collaborate—no matter the topic.

There's a natural progression, an unfolding, in developing your ability to stand confidently in all five cornerstones of your facilitation stance while in the moment. The key is building your self-awareness and self-management in relation to how you show up while you're leading a meeting.

The process of developing your practice is all about deepening your self-work. Through the practices outlined below, you'll start to stretch yourself and uncover new ways of doing things. You will start to feel more confident in how you are working with groups and teams, and you will likely find it easier to hold all five cornerstones of your facilitation stance at once.

When it comes to mastering the five cornerstones, there are more questions than answers. It is an ongoing journey of personal development and experience. The key throughout your career will be to continually deepen your self-awareness through your practice of self-reflection.

True mastery comes when you reach the point of feeling like it's time to take bigger risks with how you intervene in the group process. With the help of the following practices, you'll have a firm understanding of what you're doing and why you're doing it. You will have developed your own model for facilitation, you will know how you work with groups, and you will know how you design for intervention.

At the level of mastery, there is no need to engage in debate with other practitioners about what they do or don't do in their own facilitation processes. This is about being clear on your own model and grounded in your own practice—and understanding that the self-work needed for facilitation will be ongoing throughout your career.

Lesson 1: Work with a co-facilitator

One of the best ways to get better at the practice of facilitation is to co-facilitate. Working with someone who has less experience than you offers you a chance to mentor someone, which is one of the best ways to grow your own practice, while working with someone who has similar or more experience will likely stretch you. Groups will also receive great value from co-facilitation, as they will benefit from seeing the different approaches that each facilitator brings to the room.

When you step in front of a group, you are often showing its members your best. You are clear, confident, and outcome oriented. But a co-facilitator will be able to see the sides of fear, doubt, uncertainty, and lack of clarity in how you're handling something. They will be able to provide support in the moment, and their great feedback afterward will help you grow as a facilitator.

I think of a co-facilitator as someone who has my back. I trust them implicitly when they pick up the reins and take the group in a certain direction. But learning the dance of co-facilitation is its own practice. You will each see things differently, which means you will need to design your facilitation process with awareness around how you lead in the moment.

Designing the relationship and process of co-leading is vital to your success when sharing any leadership role. This is especially true of co-facilitating. To get the conversation started, consider having each facilitator respond to the following questions. Listen for areas where you align and areas where you differ so that you can design for the difference and create agreements for how you will handle it:

- *How do you invite more participation?*
- *How do you close off a conversation?*
- *What do you do when heated conflict or debate emerges?*
- *What do you do when someone pushes back on the process?*
- *How do you intervene? What's your style?*
- *How do you hold time? Is it important to start and end on time? What, if anything, would have you extend the meeting time?*
- *What will we do when one of us notices something happening in the room? (E.g., would we call a timeout and discuss? Would one of us name it and work with it, agreeing that the other will support? Etc.)*
- *What if one of us disagrees with what the other says or does? How will we handle it? What will our agreements be?*
- *What happens if one of us is triggered by the group?*
- *What happens if we are triggered by each other?*

Once you've heard from each other on these far-ranging topics, you get to design a facilitation that will both support the group and help you develop your personal facilitation stance. It's a win-win!

Lesson 2: Start a journaling practice and ask yourself the tough questions

Another great practice is to journal after each time you facilitate. Through this practice, you will start noticing patterns in your facilitation behaviors and default actions, which will deepen your self-awareness in the room. In turn, your growing self-awareness will support your ability to work with different kinds of groups and to help them develop the capacity and trust to work together productively and collaboratively.

There are two different, though interrelated, approaches I've found useful for a productive journaling practice. The first is relatively organic. Using self-reflection, make notes of where and when you wanted to jump out of the process and over into the content. Recall and record when you felt like *your* agenda was driving more than the group's agenda. Explore *why* you found it difficult to stand in a storm.

Ask yourself questions like:

- *What did I notice?*
- *How did I want to respond? What was behind that desire?*
- *Is this a regular occurence? If so, when do I get triggered by topics or patterns in how the group works?*
- *What biases do I bring to the team I am working with?*

When a desire to break your stance in a collaborative meeting arises, ask yourself:

- *Why did I want to offer content/stop the storm/drive my agenda?*
- *Am I trying to elevate my position in the group?*
- *Do I have a different perspective? If so, can I inquire from the group if anyone has a different perspective?*
- *What consequence would there be if I broke my stance?*
- *What would serve the group?*

When it felt like your facilitation didn't go well, ask yourself:

- *What were the facts of what was happening in the room?*

- *What were people doing?*
- *What were they saying?*
- *Now, what—specifically!— made you say this "did not go well"?*
- *What did you feel and why?*
- *What moment felt like the "tipping point" (i.e., when it started to go poorly)?*

Think about what unrealistic expectations you might be making for yourself or of others. For example, perhaps you want every person to like you at the end of the meeting. When you identify these kinds of expectations, ask yourself:

- *How do these expectations raise the stakes for you?*
- *What are you afraid the outcome will be if you "fail" to meet these expectations?*
- *What is a more realistic alternative expectation?*

With this sort of organic journaling process, the goal is simply to ask yourself the tough questions and explore them.

The second approach I've found useful when it comes to journaling is geared specifically toward becoming more aware of your own triggers. It's called the Left Hand Column Exercise, from Peter M. Senge et al., *The Fifth Discipline Fieldbook*.[11] It's about noticing when you get "hooked" by something that is said in the room and exploring the moment's effect on you and the process.

Here's how to do it: recall the specific moment in the meeting that didn't go exactly as you had hoped. Capture the context

---

11 Peter M. Senge, Art Kleiner, Charlotte Roberts, Richard B. Ross, and Bryan J. Smith, *The Fifth Discipline Fieldbook: Strategies and Tools for Building a Learning Organization* (New York: Currency, 1994), 246-252.

and your intent from that moment. Then, on one page, draw two columns.

+ *In the RIGHT hand column, write out the facts of the conversation as they actually occurred—just as a camera would have recorded it. Capture who said what.*
+ *In the LEFT hand column, describe what you were thinking and feeling but not saying.*

LEFT-HAND COLUMN (What I am thinking...)	RIGHT-HAND COLUMN (What is Said, Just the Facts...)

Then, consider and journal on the following questions:

+ *What were you trying to accomplish?*
+ *What was your intention?*
+ *If you've familiarized yourself with the action modes of Structural Dynamics, code the conversation into MOVE, FOLLOW, BYSTAND, and OPPOSE. What patterns do you notice?*

- *Why did you hold back and not voice what was in your left-hand column?*
- *What assumptions were you making about the situation or the other people in the room?*
- *What got in the way of you acting differently?*
- *What would you do differently next time?*
- *What part did you play in the outcome?*
- *How does this experience inform your learning about your practice of facilitation?*

Here's an example of what this exercise might look like:

LEFT-HAND COLUMN (What I was thinking.)	RIGHT-HAND COLUMN (What was said. Just the facts.)
I hope this goes well ... this team has been *so* resistant to meetings like this. Oh, here we go… Why can't they just try something new? She does this every time, always opposing any new ideas. He's just saying that because he agrees with her every time. They just don't trust me! Why can't they believe that I know what I'm talking about? If I don't shut this down soon, we will spend the whole time debating the purpose of the meeting and accomplish nothing. If that happens then I will be viewed as a failure	**Me:** The purpose of our meeting today is to reflect on how we have been working over the past month. We want to see where we have opportunities for learning and define one action we will take to improve how we work. **Jill:** I have a question. I'm not sure why we need all of this time to have a conversation. Can't we just ask everyone to write down a suggestion and vote on it? Seems like it would take less time. **Isaiah:** I agree. I think this is not a great use of our time. **Me:** Well, Scrum says that retrospectives are important to the team. Since we're implementing agile, I think we need to try these meetings out and see what we get.

Ultimately, this kind of journaling is about noticing when you start to make it about you rather than keeping your attention on the group. We all have stories that guide our biases and responses, and, depending on the team or organization we're working with, they can become more present in the moment and influence our choices. Cultivating self-awareness is our first and best line of defense against slipping out of our facilitation stance.

But don't forget: the key to developing your practice is, of course, to have patience. Learning to maintain neutrality while holding the group's agenda, for example, is like building a muscle. You will grow and improve over time. Over time, however, when you deepen your self-awareness through reflection, you cultivate your ability to notice in real time when you've faltered in your facilitation stance. In turn, you will start to develop your capacity for course correcting in the moment.

Awareness precedes choice precedes change.

Lesson 3: Change "roles" in order to share your opinions and perspectives

As the facilitator, you will absolutely have a point of view and an opinion. In fact, the mental models you use to understand how teams develop, what makes agility work, how teams reach high performance, and your own experiences will all highly inform your perspective in the room and the questions you decide to ask of the group. And that's a good thing!

The key is to be constantly asking yourself: how can I *best* support the team based on where they are now?

The trick to sharing your opinions and perspectives is learning to share in a way that does not make you right and the team wrong. If there is a topic of conversation happening in the room that you either know something about or you have information and context that the group seems to be missing, then turn to the group for guidance:

- *"I think I have some information about this topic. Would it be helpful for me to share it right now?"*
- *"This seems challenging right now. May I offer some ideas..."*
- *"I could give you a quick overview of the applicable agile principle and some options that you might try..."*
- *I could provide you with some references to check out for the future..."*

By asking, you're letting the group remain the content owners. *They* can decide in the moment if they want more information or not. Be willing and open for the team to say yes or no, and move forward from there. If they say yes, then signal to yourself and to the group that you are stepping out of the role of facilitator and into content. One way to do this is, for example, is to sit down if you've been standing. Once you've stepped out of the facilitator role, share your content, expertise, or advice.

Everyone will have their own way of bringing their viewpoint into the meeting. As you develop your facilitation skills, you get to find the way that works for *you*. How you want to say things in the room so the team is at choice, so that you are not overly driving them in a direction they did not want to go. How you want to incorporate your viewpoint with high interest and low attachment. To help you figure out what works best for you, I recommend simply trying out different approaches and then asking for impact feedback. In the moment, you might ask if what you tried was helpful. Or, you might wait until the end of the meeting to ask what impact your sharing had on the individual participants.

When you really begin to understand when and how to share your point of view, you will be living your own model of an agile mindset. After all, part of your role is understanding how to adapt and change to what the team needs. Sometimes a team needs more guidance. Other times, your role might be more facilitative. As you develop your facilitation skills, you will learn to tell the difference. Moreover, because you've learned to honor the wisdom of the group, you will have created a space where they feel able to *tell* you what they need when they need it.

Be clear, for yourself, that *training* and *facilitation* are different skills. They are different stances that are used to achieve different outcomes. Training is about conveying information. Facilitation is about enabling collective outcomes. Ask the team what *they* think would be most helpful to them in the moment, and trust them to guide you in what they need. If they need a 15-minute "chalk talk" with you at the front of the room wearing your "trainer" hat, then do that for them. Just recognize that this is a different role and make sure you return to your facilitator role afterward. And don't hang out in that role for too long. Be concise, then step back into facilitation.

The point is to trust that the team knows what they need—and they don't need you to jump six steps ahead and make a decision for them. If you feel like it's a disservice to the topic or the group for your voice to be missing from the conversation, consider asking someone else to step into the role of facilitator so that you can join in as a full participant.

By bringing clarity to the role you are playing (facilitator, trainer, advisor, content contributor, leader, etc.) you signal to the group that you can be trusted and counted on to do what you said you would do at the start. With this clarity and trust, they will also know when you are clearly in the space of neutrality—even if you have your opinion or perspective to share.

Lesson 4: Work with a supervisor

That's right! No matter how developed your practice, your facilitation skills can *always* be deepened through outside perspective. That's why I often recommend that facilitators and team coaches get supervision or work with a coach of their own throughout their career—not just when they're starting out.

Supervision provides a much different kind of outside perspective than is gleaned from co-facilitation. It's a concept that comes from the field of professional coaching and draws on best practices from psychotherapy and counseling. In the process of supervision for facilitation, you bring recordings of your facilitations to your supervisor and reflect on the work together. They help you gain key insights into how you're working with the team and help you identify how your blind spots—things that you might not be noticing in the room—are impacting the work you do with groups.

Supervision can happen individually or in small groups. In fact, surrounding yourself with other facilitators who can provide good feedback is a great way to get even more from the process—no matter how long you've been doing this work. They help you develop your inner presence and awareness, which, in turn, deepens your capacity to lead high-stakes meetings.

By this point, you are already journaling and self-reflecting as a cornerstone of your facilitation practice. A supervisor or coach takes you even further in your work. Because no matter how developed your practice, your facilitation skills can *always* be deepened through outside perspective.

Lesson 5: Intervene to break patterns

Sometimes what a group needs is something to disrupt their familiar habits. Yet disrupting habits, naming things that the group is unaware of, or surfacing topics they might not want to address comes with high stakes—for you and for them.

As we discussed earlier in this book, it can be useful to *invite* and *encourage* opposition because there is value in surfacing differing viewpoints. However, you can also create a generative kind of storm by thinking creatively when it comes to disrupting people's basic preconceptions about what a meeting should look like.

In most of my work with teams, I remove the tables from the room and put chairs in a circle instead. Why? Because circles are the strongest shape. They foster greater connection and allow people to see everyone else in the room. Everyone is equal. Plus, it breaks the pattern of what it looks like to "come to a meeting."

Think about it: how often do you attend a meeting and feel pulled in multiple directions? Let's say you have a report that's due in two hours, and now you also have a meeting that you know will take up at least one of those hours. It's not an optimal situation, but you have to get the report done! So, you march off to the meeting with your laptop in hand. You sit down at the table, open your report, and begin working—all while trying to listen to the meeting, too.

Multitasking is an illusion, and it sends the message that "this is not important to me" or "my time is more valuable than yours." This is why we intervene and remove the tables. We want people to experience what's truly possible if they fully show up to a meeting, connect, and engage—even when they're stressed about everything on their plate.

The impact of arranging chairs in a circle is slightly uncomfortable for some. For others, it sends them into high-stakes mode. The impact shows up for people in all kinds of ways, and it's often directed at the facilitators. Sometimes, we get referred to as "those touchy-feely people." Some people roll their eyes when they walk into the room. But regardless of the response, the result is that people sit down in a circle and engage differently—even when it's uncomfortable.

The chairs send the message that this is going to be a different kind of meeting, and as facilitators with mastery over our practice, we are prepared to weather whatever storm that might bring.

My co-facilitator and I ran an experiment once. We let a team we had been working with lead their own meeting and we just observed. They went back to the tables. Out came the laptops and, sure enough, the quality of their conversation and their decisions changed. In fact, they didn't reach a decision at all in that meeting. Stinging comments were lobbed in every direction, and the group left the meeting with open issues and not much resolution.

Creating perturbation by interrupting patterns does not have to be a massive intervention. And it should never be about shaming or blaming. But when done thoughtfully to bring awareness to what's happening in the room, it can make space for generative, collaborative thinking that might otherwise be hard to access.

Lesson 6: Articulate what's happening in the group

Being neutral does not mean that you are passively standing by and watching. Not only do you own the process and make process moves, you are also playing a role in helping a group see how they are working and understand what might be getting in their way. You are actively helping them have more productive conversations. There is nothing passive about it.

However, when you feel compelled to contribute *content*, it's often because you see something happening in the group that you want to fix. This is active, but it's not necessarily neutral. Instead of interjecting new content, try naming what's happening in the group's process or dynamics. This action helps build the team's competency for seeing their own dynamics. It helps them become more self-sufficient over time, rely less on the facilitator, and take responsibility and ownership for their outcomes.

Of course, this is easier said than done, which is why maintaining neutrality and honoring the wisdom of the group are pieces of your facilitation stance that will need ongoing attention to develop.

When you have the impulse to jump into the content, practice using your model for team dynamics. Name what you see, without judgement. In Structural Dynamics, this is the action of Bystand.

You might say:

- *"I notice we've been talking about this same subject for fifteen minutes. Is this helpful? If not, what would move us forward?"*
- *"There are three different subjects in the conversation right now. What's the one you would like to talk about first?"*
- *"This proposal has come up in conversation three times. What do you want to do with it?"*

Naming what's happening is a way to help the group take more responsibility for how they are interacting and helps them build collaborative competence.

If the conversation seems to be moving more in the direction of conflict—a storm—you might say something like:

♦ *"I'm noticing a lot of energy on this topic. I hear two differ-ent perspectives about which way to go, but I hear alignment around delivering a product that is useful to our customers. What do others see?"*

In this example you are helping to name what's happening and bridge the competing ideas. You are helping the two sides find alignment on *something*, even if it's at a value level, so they can build from there.

You might also find yourself in a situation where you're not really sure what's going on in a group, but your group dynamic "spidey senses" tell you that something's not quite right. In moments like this, you might even find yourself starting to make up stories about what's happening. If the group is really silent, for example, you might tell yourself that they don't understand what's being talked about, or they really don't like what you've asked them to do. When you start using stories to fill in the gaps, it's time to check it out with the group.

You might say:

♦ *"So, I'm noticing that everyone is very quiet right now. What's happening in this moment?"*

You might need to exercise your muscle to create space and allow silence. You should remain in silence until you get uncom-fortable, and then remain in silence about 3–4 times longer. I know! It's tough. But people need time to think and respond to a question that they are likely not often asked. It can throw the group off guard. Rachel Smith, a dear colleague, suggests grab-bing a beverage—if you have one—and take a very long sip while you wait for a response.

The key to developing your practice is to know your own stories and trigger points. Know what brings your self-preservation and defensive instincts out. Become aware of them through your journaling and reflection practices so that you can see them coming *before* they grab hold and start running the show.

Lesson 7: Develop your model for facilitation

The notion of model building, which we talked about in relation to agile adaptability in Chapter 5, applies to you in your facilitation practice as well. This book is intended to be a thought-provoking guide to get you started on your path. Eventually, you will begin to feel constrained by some of the guidance offered here. And when you do, it's a good indicator that you're ready to define your *own* stance for facilitation.

One of the first cornerstones you will likely find yourself revisiting as you begin to define your own model is the idea of maintaining neutrality. I get asked about this one frequently. "Can I ever get 'good enough' to hold both the process *and* the content?" Earlier in this book, I provided guidance on how to stick to the process even when it feels difficult. In the previous section of this chapter, you learned how to develop the skill of remaining neutral while sharing your own point of view. Now, the question becomes, What is *your* model for facilitation when it comes to neutrality? This is your time to explore.

One's relative ability to hold both process and content depends on the complexity of the issue and the importance of the meeting overall. There are times and places where you *can* do both, and when you *can* hold both roles. If this is something you want to explore, I recommend revisiting the exercise of "Sharing Neutral Leadership" (Lesson 3 of Chapter 1: Maintaining Neutrality).

The success of your practice will be as much about the group dynamic and group trust as it will be about your own skill set.

One group I work with has gone to full neutrality over time. Each team member has been finding their own version of what neutrality means and learning about when and how to offer their opinion or perspective. Individually, they are increasingly able to hold both roles in their meetings. Depending on the role that facilitation plays in a group—as well as in the organization overall—this may very well constitute "mastery." But perhaps a more meaningful perspective on mastery is not that it is the ability to engage in both content and process, but that it is the development of a true and deep understanding of why you might *want* to—as well as the skills to self-manage accordingly.

Consider journaling and self-reflection on the following questions:

- *What do I believe about teams and how they work best?*
- *What's my point of view about effective and ineffective group dynamics?*
- *What's the role of the facilitator in supporting group outcomes?*
- *How would I define my personal stance on neutrality?*
- *What are the circumstances where I might provide content?*
- *How do I provide content so it's clear to both myself and the team that I am stepping out of neutrality?*
- *When might I hand a process over to someone else in the meeting?*

As you find your own way and develop your own model for facilitation, self awareness will continue to be the key. You'll find a natural cadence and volume for how much content you may bring in versus how much to focus on owning the process and maintaining 100% neutrality. But no matter what balance you find, always be clear about boundaries. As you wear different hats, just remember my earlier guidance, because it will still apply: be sure to make it transparent for both you and the team which one is on your head at any given time.

CONCLUSION

If you, as a facilitator, find yourself in the space of being singularly responsible and accountable for a team's success and outcomes, you are in a dangerous place. It doesn't matter how developed or masterful your practice.

Once, when I was introducing the concepts of facilitation to a group of new facilitators inside an organization, I noticed collective resistance from them as the week unfolded. It was especially apparent when we would talk about the concept of storms—the presence of conflict or opposition in the room. I realized that they had a narrative around conflict in groups: they saw it as "career limiting," meaning that if they were in a meeting that "went off the rails," they would be held accountable for a poor design and execution.

Throughout your career, you will likely experience this kind of thinking, either from yourself or from others. As a new facilitator, practicing the five cornerstones of your facilitation stance will help you navigate it. As a masterful facilitator, you will have a clear understanding of how to head it off from the get-go. Using the practices introduced in this chapter, you will be able to recognize if this belief is one of *your* triggering narratives, you will have developed the ability to articulate what's happening in the room to get at what's really going on, and you will know how to intervene to break patterns of limiting thinking and interactions.

What it comes down to, is that understanding the role that group process and dynamics play in creating lasting and meaningful outcomes is vital to being able to navigate these kinds of narratives when they emerge. Everything you do will be in service of helping the group overcome them so that they can have the real conversation and collaborate toward the productive outcome. This is why, for example, you know to design with the sponsor and the team ahead of the meeting in order to create an effective meeting container. It lets you see how they might view and handle conflict and its importance in being able to cultivate a space where genuine learning and innovative thinking can take place. It's why you've become clear about your point of view when it comes to how teams collaborate best together, and you know how and when to share this perspective within the group process.

There is a collective (systemic) responsibility for the outcomes that team's produce. It's not your job, as the facilitator, to own the responsibility for the outcome. Rather, your job is to own the part you play while holding the group responsible for the part *they* play. As you develop and eventually master your facilitation stance, you will find yourself more and more comfortable in the collective ownership of outcomes.

> Here is my final word of guidance as you embark on your journey: remember that responsibility in facilitation means owning your part and helping the group own theirs.

CONCLUSION:

Beyond Facilitation

The greatest way to change a culture is by changing the way it meets.

~Patrick Lencioni

*T*he *Art and Science of Facilitation* is a story about collaboration. It's a story about understanding who you are being when you show up in the room, and it's about thinking practically and conceptually about how to show up productively.

> It's about believing that language is at the core of everything.

For those of you who are new to facilitation, this book offers:

- *Beliefs and mindsets that support true collaboration*
- *A way of thinking about your own leadership beyond telling others what to do or solving the problem for them*

> ◆ *A way of including all voices in a process without it becoming overdone or winding up stuck*
> ◆ *A vision for facilitation that goes beyond just orchestrating the meeting, ordering snacks, and taking notes*

For those of you in an agile environment, this book offers a way of being agile that goes beyond the basics of agile values, principles, and practices. It is designed to help you focus on what you bring as a leader and how you show up in your work. This is the difference between *doing* agile and **being** agile. After all, agile development, at its most basic level, calls for frequent communication and collaboration. There are thousands of ways to go about executing agile practices, and there are plenty of places to get training in agility. But the skills you're developing in this book will take you *beyond* the basic tools and practices to get to the heart of what's really going to make a difference in how a team functions.

This book is about grounding yourself in the dance of collaboration.

If I only get to be in the room with someone for three days, then I want to spend as much time as possible knee-deep in the experience of what it means to cultivate and hold a space that allows for learning, insights, and meaningful action. I want to listen to what's being said and not said, turn down my own thoughts so I can hear what others are thinking, and trust that there is wisdom within the group. In my experience, this is what it means to be an effective, agile facilitator.

Agility will come by our ability to be in deeper dialogue about what's happening and what's needed in the product, the team, the organization, etc. Our collective ability to have dialogue will come with greater awareness and some support in getting there.

In other words, agility might come from practices, but without dialogue and collaboration it won't be true agility.

If nothing else, this book stands for two simple ideas:

* ✦ *When you are facilitating, collaboration begins with you*
* ✦ *When you are facilitating, you must manage yourself*

And yet, ultimately, it's not about you at all. That's the twist! Facilitation begins with you, but it's about taking yourself and your ego *out* of the equation in order to be in service to a greater cause. It's about finding collective wisdom, talking about what really matters, and bringing the conversation into the room.

To help you navigate the challenges of upholding these ideas, each chapter you have read has introduced a key principle for effective facilitation, as well as guidance for how to practice and develop the self-awareness you will need to tap into along the way.

It's not easy. Human systems often feel like they don't *naturally* create space for collaboration. But if we focus on the human system through communication—by engaging in a *dialogue*— then we are likely to develop new ways of working, see solutions to presenting problems differently, and uncover new ways of working.

So, in concluding this introduction to the five cornerstones stances that comprise theAgile Team Facilitation Stance, let's look beyond. Let's look at dialogue.

Dialogue holds the key to many of the complex challenges that exist in teams and organizations today. It is, in short, collective meaning making. It is the space where groups organically bring all four actions (Move, Follow, Oppose and Bystand), and where every member is engaged in the dialogue practices of Voice, Listen, Respect, and Suspend.[12] The facilitation principles offered in this book are a great launching pad for starting to focus on dialogue, because holding dialogue starts with creating a container and inviting a group into a dialogic process. Yet hosting dialogue requires, from both the facilitator and the team, a set of beliefs beyond what's offered here. It is the next stage of development in creating the most generative and co-creative spaces.

My observation about teams, particularly top leadership teams, is that their inability to dialogue about meaningful topics and emerge with new thinking and ideas is the single greatest impediment to agility, adaptive businesses, and innovative thinking. I've come to believe that we spend a good deal of time hiding and pretending in organizations, and it is not possible to enter into and be in dialogue without *truth*. Getting teams, especially top teams, to be honest, vulnerable, and candid with one other is a significant lift.

But the generative feeling and effective outcomes that emerge when true dialogue happens are awakening and energizing. I've been in the room with teams where the differing points of view were so palpable and the moral judgment so strong that you could feel it. Yet I've watched these teams enter into dialogue, listening and inquiring of one another and voicing what's true for them, until something new happens. In these moments, the energy in the room discernibly shifts from defiance and judgment to understanding and clarity. And that's when completely new ideas emerge. From there, the energy and action become unstoppable. Moreover, the alignment and clarity can be sustainable enough for teams to continue the process of trying new things far into the future.

---

12   See William Isaacs, *Dialogue: The Art of Thinking Together* (New York: Currency, 1999).

Should you choose to venture into the world of dialogue, bring everything you've learned about neutrality and group wisdom and amp it up. In the practice of facilitation, there is quite a bit of power that resides with the facilitator. Even though it's been granted to the facilitator by the group, the facilitator is still leading the process. In dialogue, there is no leader. The power dynamics are flattened, and you are *in* the process with the group. You are no longer separate.

Dialogue requires container building and establishing principles for how the group will work together. There is no agenda. There are no specific outcomes. There is no decision-making framework. Instead, there is space for emergence, learning, a new level of understanding, and new thought. Attention is given to the quality of presence—the ability to listen deeply and to be with and respect difference. Equal attention is given to each person voicing, with respect, what is true for them.[13]

Changing the way we engage with others, from creating space for more conversation to cultivating the skills of dialogue, offers us richer opportunities for collaborative thinking. It offers the chance to get in the car rather than running down the road saying we're too busy to stop for a ride. Our communication and behavior lay the tracks that everything else sits on top of. If our actions and behaviors don't match our values, the train won't go far. And its facilitators who can change the way we interact in day-to-day communication. They can design a space that invites collaborative conversation and generative dialogue,

---

13   For further reading and learning on dialogue, see Paul Lawrence and Sarah Hill, et al., *The Tao of Dialogue* (New York: Routledge, 2019); Williams Issacs, *Dialogue: the Art of Thinking Together* (New York: Currency, 1999); David Bohm, *On Dialogue* (New York: Routledge, 1996); Annette Simmons, *A Safe Space for Dangerous Truths: Using Dialogue to Overcome Fear and Distrust at Work* (New York: AMACOM, 1999).

which in turn creates greater efficiency, greater understanding, and greater facility for addressing the *real* problem—not just the perceived problem.

In the end, this all about conversations. The culture in our organizations is shaped by the language we use and the stories we tell about what's helpful and not helpful. What will be rewarded and valued and what will be discarded or not appreciated. Therefore, the highest and best use of a leader's time is to cultivate a culture where conversations and collaboration are valued. Where leading collaborative conversations is viewed as a craft and a competency worth developing. Where people are rewarded for engaging in honest dialogue so that teams—and ultimately the organization—are aligned in a way that they can use conversations to move forward. Where they hold the belief that the most important aspect of solving complex problems is to engage the right people in *dialogue.*

Conversations are the core of leading sustainable change. It's not always sexy. It's not always glamorous. But if you're in an organization that is struggling to find its way in agility, if your teams are stuck trying to create *process*-led change rather than change that begins with our basic interactive behaviors, then facilitation—and the conversations it enables—is the answer.

Wherever you are starting from in your facilitation journey, the practice and development of the five facilitation principles will deepen your capacity to create space for collaboration and communication with others. I hope that this resource will be a stepping stone for you, and that, as you continue your journey, you remember that your greatest failures can also be your greatest lessons—if you allow it.

My highest dream is that we are all collectively changing the way organizations engage in the art of communication and collaboration. If nothing else, I hope this book has helped you share the same dream.

RECOMMENDED READING

Lyssa Adkins, *Coaching Agile Teams: A Companion for Scrum-Masters, Agile Coaches and Project Managers in Transition* (Boston: Addison Wesley, 2010).

Chris Argysis, "Double Loop Learning in Organizations," *Harvard Business Review*, September 1977.

David Bohm, On Dialogue (New York: Routledge, 1996).

Larry Dressler, Standing in the Fire: Leading High-Heat Meetings with Clarity, Calm, and Courage (San Francisco: Berrett-Koehler Publishers, 2010).

Carol Dweck, *Mindset: The Psychology of Success* (New York: Random House, 2006).

Amy C. Edmondson, *The Fearless Organization: Creating Psychological Safety in the Workplace for Learning, Innovation, and Growth* (Hoboken: John Wiley & Sons, 2019).

William Isaacs, *Dialogue: The Art of Thinking Together* (New York: Currency, 1999).

David Kantor, *Reading the Room: Group Dynamics for Coaches and Leaders* (San Francisco: Jossey-Bass, 2012).

Henry Kimsey-House, Karen Kimsey-House, Phillip Sandahl, and Laura Whitworth, *Co-Active Coaching: Changing Business, Transforming Lives* (Boston: Nicholas Brealey Publishing, 2011)0.

James D. and Wendy Kayser Kirkpatrick, *Four Levels of Training Evaluation* (Alexandria: ATD Press, 2016).

Paul Lawrence and Sarah Hill, et al., The Tao of Dialogue (New York: Routledge, 2019).

Roger Schwarz, The Skilled Facilitator: A Comprehensive Resource for Consultants, Facilitators, Managers, Trainers, and Coaches (San Francisco: Jossey-Bass, 2002).

Roger Schwarz, Anne Davidson, Peg Carlson, Sue McKinney, et al., The Skilled Facilitator Fieldbook: Tips, Tools, and Tested Methods for Consultants, Facilitators, Managers, Trainers, and Coaches (San Francisco: Jossey-Bass, 2005).

Peter M. Senge, Art Kleiner, Charlotte Roberts, Richard B. Ross, Bryan J. Smith, The Fifth Discipline Fieldbook: Strategies and Tools for Building a Learning Organization (New York: Currency, 1994).

ABOUT THE AUTHOR

Marsha Acker has been drawn to the promise and power of using conversations to bridge divides and help teams solve complex and difficult challenges that have no easy answers. Marsha's thinking about how to approach change was highly informed by learning to embrace the key values of agile early in her career.

Her thinking about large-scale organizational change shifted significantly in 2002 as she worked with a government organization making a significant structural change. It was in this process that she learned both the difficulty of talking about the real change and the importance of how conversations and shared meaning and understanding change the nature of the outcome for both the leadership team and the organization.

Over the last eighteen years she has worked with leaders and organizations to bring the transformative nature of the competencies of facilitation and coaching to organizations seeking agility, innovation, and leadership for the 21st century.

Collaboration is rarely straightforward or easy, but it's worth it. The investment in developing the ability as a leader to truly be facilitative and create a culture that fosters collaboration has rewards that exceed the investment. And if you let it, growing your competence in facilitation will grow and stretch you as a leader, every time.

Marsha is a professional facilitator and executive coach with 25 years of experience supporting leaders as they tackle complex challenges and lead change in their organizations. The founder and CEO of TeamCatapult, she uses system thinking, Structural Dynamics, dialogue and agility to help teams collaborate and align with clarity, purpose, and vision.

She and her colleagues at TeamCatapult are dedicated to the mission of helping Scrum masters, agile coaches, and leaders grow their competency in facilitation and coaching in order to lead change and cultivate effective teams. Join them at Team-Catapult.com.

For more information and free resources, go to the book website, ArtandScienceofFacilitation.com.

ACKNOWLEDGEMENTS

This book is the result of a twenty-six-year evolution of my own model for facilitation. It represents a series of ongoing conversations I have had with myself and many, many others about what creates the conditions for collective wisdom and intelligence. As with any journey there are so many beautiful souls that you meet along the path that it's hard to articulate the impact and contribution they have each made.

For starters, for every colleague, partner, and client—if we have worked together in some capacity, just know that our conversations, questions, constraints, and relationships have informed my thinking about facilitation in some way. Thank you.

To Mark Franz and Jeff Hackert for the kick in the seat of the pants during a late-night conversation over dinner at the agile conference many years ago. It was your feedback and encouragement that solidified my decision to actually make this happen. Thank you!

To Joe Dietzel, my very first manager, who believed in me and my crazy vision for facilitation when, all those years ago, I wanted to bring users and developers together so they could listen and learn from one another and develop better software. And to Susan Stalick and Dorien Andrews who first taught me about facilitation and different ways to engage groups. These folks, and others like them, ignited my passion for collaboration and a facilitative style of leadership.

To Ahmed Sidky, for your partnership as the first iteration of the agile team facilitation stance was emerging, and to Michael Spayd and Lyssa Adkins for our collective conversations in the early days. We dreamed what would be possible when the world of agility had broad access to the powerful skills of facilitation and coaching and crafted the first ever learning objectives for Agile Coaching. Those conversations grew me and my thinking, and I appreciate our continued relationships.

My coach training with the Coaches Training Institute profoundly changed my life. It took only three short days in my first Fundamentals class to realize I wanted to look at the world in a completely different way than I had been. Henry Kimsey-House, Karen Kimsey-House, and the CTI faculty, thank you for inspiring me and informing my model for looking deeper into the mindset of facilitation.

To Doug Stone and Shelia Heen for the most wonderful "Business Book Writing Bootcamp" retreat in Rhode Island. I learned so much about the craft and journey of writing a business book. I will forever remember the stories you shared of your own journey in writing. I deeply appreciated the time to be in space together and the individual space to write and create. To my amazing colleagues and authors from that week—Phil Buchanan, Diana Patton, Sarah Hill, Kathryn Stanely, Peter Hiddema—a special thank you for enduring the reviews of very early drafts of this book and for your feedback.

Sarah Hill, with her support and coaching guidance, as well as the learning I did with Tony Melville, Donata Caira, Kathryn

Stanley, Gillien Todd, Kieran White and Marcelo Agolti, have greatly impacted my understanding about structural dynamics and model building. The dialogue, ongoing friendships, and collaborative partnerships I've gained from this supportive and challenging group of colleagues continues to shape my thinking.

And, of course, I would like to thank David Kantor, whose work on structural dynamics has profoundly informed the way I think about and see group dynamics—from the important role structure plays on the outcomes we get to our role as facilitator, coach, leader, or practitioner in "doing less harm and knowing the harm you can do." The time spent talking about epistemic failure informs much of my thinking to this day.

Stories are great, but when they reside only in your head they are not very durable and their impact is limited. I'm pretty sure this book would not exist if not for my editor, Elena Abbott. She reframed my whole perspective on writing from a laborious and difficult task to a practice that I now do with joy, flow, and fun. Her questions, challenges, and reframes guided my sometimes murky thinking and helped me fully appreciate the perspective that I have and articulate the message that I want to share. She is an unwavering, steady, and thoughtful guide, and my work with her was joyus!

To Alex Thomas, who took my vision for a cover and made it sing. I am known to be picky about design look and feel, and he created a design that I just love!

To all of my colleagues at TeamCatapult who have been on various stages of this journey with me and who have shifted and shaped my thinking about the practice of facilitation in numerous untold ways—Larissa Caruso, Antoinette Coetzee, Jeff Hackert, Kay Harper, David Levine, Kari McLeod, Laurie Reuben, William Strydom, and Leslie Zucker—deepest gratitude to you all. The support of Trish Hallmark, Patti Ciccone,

Jennifer Judd, Anne Popolizio, Dorien Morin-van Dam, and Dallas Travers has been pivotal to the work we do.

My deepest gratitude and appreciation goes to my family. My mom, Elizabeth, taught me to persevere and find something to appreciate in every moment, which she continues even today as she lives with Alzheimers. My dad, Don, who taught me to find the humor in life and not take myself so seriously. My beautiful and loving daughter, Lauren, who teaches me something about myself every day and makes me grateful that I get to be her mom! And finally, my husband, Don, for whom I don't have enough words. He is my partner, friend, lover, supporter, speaker of truth (when needed, even if not wanted), motivator when I fall behind or get in my head too much, and overall life champion. He is a kind, generous, loving, multi-faceted Renaissance man who can do anything or be anything when he puts his mind to it. His unwavering, never hesitant, always caring love, support, and belief in me and what I want to do is the reason I have accomplished the things that I have done—this book included. I am eternally grateful for having him in my life.

"You and me together we could do anything, baby"
- Dave Matthews

And to you, my readers. Thank you for taking a further step along your own facilitation journey. It's courageous work with the potential for widespread, meaningful impact. I wish you the best as you begin to develop your own model for facilitation.

Made in the USA
Middletown, DE
28 March 2021